AN HISTORICAL ESSAY

ON THE

DRESS

OF THE

ANCIENT AND MODERN IRISH

TO WHICH IS SUBJOINED
A MEMOIR ON THE
ARMOUR AND WEAPONS
OF THE IRISH

The Naval & Military Press Ltd

published in association with

ROYAL ARMOURIES

Published by
The Naval & Military Press Ltd
Unit 10 Ridgewood Industrial Park,
Uckfield, East Sussex,
TN22 5QE England
Tel: +44 (0) 1825 749494
Fax: +44 (0) 1825 765701
www.naval-military-press.com

in association with

ROYAL
ARMOURIES

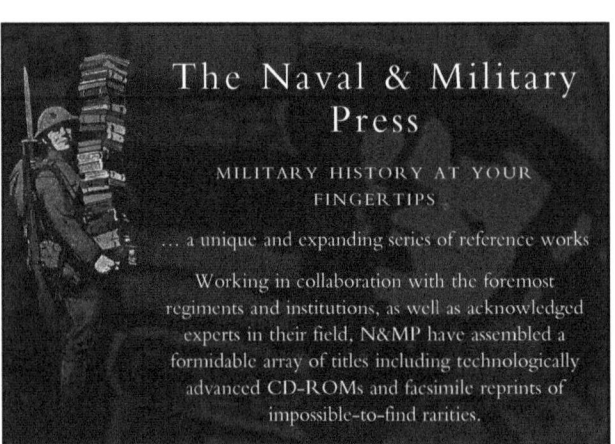

In reprinting in facsimile from the original, any imperfections are inevitably reproduced and the quality may fall short of modern type and cartographic standards.

PREFACE.

He, who undertakes to elucidate the Antiquities of Ireland, no longer engages in an ungrateful task. The Spirit of literary enquiry is gone abroad in this kingdom, and whoever advances to meet her, is sure to win her smiles. It was not, however, this flattering hope that seduced me again before the tribunal of the public. Numbered with the Royal Academicians of my native country, I deemed it a duty incumbent on me to employ my talents, such as they are, in promoting the object of their union.

The flattering reception with which the Essay on the Irish Dress, in its original state of crudeness, was honoured by that learned body, induced me to consider the subject more deeply and more extensively. Thus animated

animated in the purfuit of information, I left no means untried to obtain it. I vifited the couch of the aged, and patiently liftened to " the tale of other times"; I trimmed the midnight lamp over many a dry annalift, and pored with unremitting attention on many a mufty manufcript; I explored the mouldering walls and " long founding ifles" of cloiftered fanes, for figures illuftrative of my fubject,—nay, I even unbarred the gates of death, and entered the tomb in queft of evidences. With what fuccefs thofe enquiries were attended, the Public are now to determine.

But before they decide, it is neceffary I fhould vouch the authenticity of my graphic authorities. In order to this I fhall only fay, that feveral of the drawings were made under my own eye, and the reft executed by perfons incapable of deceiving him whom they honor with their friendfhip. But as the attempts of fculpture in Ireland before the invafion of the Englifh, were extremely rude, it may perhaps be objected to fome of my drawings that they exhibit Englifh modes of drefs. This I readily admit. But as thefe modes prevailed here, either amongft fettlers or natives, they neceffarily

fell

PREFACE.

fell in with my general defign. Sepulchral monuments (it has been juftly obferved) are fo many records of their refpective ages.

However ardent I may have been in the purfuit of information, I feldom ventured beyond the Chriftian Æra, awed by the fettled gloom that clouded the preceding ages. But I would not have it inferred from this confeffion, that I confider the Pagan ages of Ireland as wrapped in impenetrable opacity. Difguifed by prejudice, or tortured into deformity by enthufiafm, Irifh hiftory, for fome ages, hath worn a forbidding afpect; but touched by the Ithurielan fpear, I do not defpair of feeing her ftart up in an engaging form.

It was hinted to me by a friend who perufed my manufcript, that I dwell with too much energy on the oppreffions of the Englifh, treading fometimes with an heavy ftep, on afhes not yet cold. But however thankful for the hint, I cannot fubfcribe to his opinion. I have only related unexaggerated hiftoric truths. This was my duty, and from this duty no mortal frown can make me fwerve.

swerve. "Personne (says Fleury) n'est obligé d'écrire "l'histoire; mais quiconque l'entrepend, s'engage à dire la "vérité toute entiere." But the wrongs of the English only live now in the page of history. Mingling their blood with ours, that brave people have conciliated our affections. We have taken them to our arms, and stifled the remembrance of their oppressions in a warm embrace.

As no historical compilation of the nature of the present work could be completed by the single efforts of one man---and he engaged in a variety of pursuits--- I was necessitated to solicit foreign aid. Several of those learned friends who assisted me on a former occasion, kindly and assiduously promoted the present work; particularly, the ingenious Mr. BEAUFORD of Athy, RALPH OUSLEY esquire, Colonel VALLANCEY, and the reverend EDWARD LEDWICH. The reverend DANIEL AUGUSTUS BEAUFORT too, during his peregrinations through this kingdom for the laudable purpose of collecting materials for *A Civil and Ecclesiastical Map of Ireland*, employed his pencil in my service. To the pencil also of my Brother and another ingenious kinsman, I have

have many obligations. With them I have visited several remains of antiquity, availing myself of their skill in drawing, while they joined with me in admiring and lamenting many beautiful yet neglected monuments of ages which we are taught to deem barbarous. To the right honourable the Earl of HILLSBOROUGH my thanks are due, and here publickly offered for a curious communication. Several other noblemen and gentlemen have just claims to my grateful acknowledgements.

But it is to the Countess of MOIRA my thanks are most particularly due. " While adorning courts with her presence, and diffusing elegance by her example," her thoughts were still bent on the acquirement of knowledge: Her studies embraced every subject of polite literature, and her mind became replete with useful and elegant information. From the emanations of such a mind, what might not be expected! Condescending to honor me with her correspondence during the progress of this work, there are few pages in either of the Essays, which I am now offering to the Public, that cannot boast some obligation to her Ladyship.

CONTENTS.

ERRATA.

Page.	Line.	Note.	
14,	13,		*for* protected, *read* protects.
22,		*(y)*	*for* the royal crown, *r.* a golden crown.
42,	16,		*for* difovered, *r.* difcovered.
46,		*(d)*	*for* Holinghed, *r.* Holinfhed, *paſſim*.
52,			*dele* Note *(t)*; the term *ſhorn*, as there uſed, being equivocal.

CONTENTS.

An Historical Essay on the Dress of the Ancient and Modern Irish.

A Memoir on the Armour and Weapons of the Irish.

APPENDIX.

[No. I.]

An Account of the Customs, Manners, and Dress of the Inhabitants of The Rosses. In a Letter to the Author. By the Rev. A―― B――.

[No. II.]

CONTENTS.

[No. II.]

A descriptive Catalogue of Irish Implements of War in the Collection of Ralph Ousley, Esq; M. R. I. A. In a Letter to the Author.

[No. III.]

An Account of three Relicks of Antiquity found in Ireland.

[No. IV.]

An Act that the Natives of this Realm shall have Bowes and other Armour. (10 Hen. VII.)

[No. V.]

A List of the Plates illustrating this Work, with Observations.

AN

HISTORICAL ESSAY

ON THE

DRESS

OF THE

ANCIENT AND MODERN IRISH.

AN HISTORICAL ESSAY

ON THE

DRESS OF THE IRISH.

ADDRESSED TO THE RIGHT HONOURABLE THE

EARL OF CHARLEMONT:

My Lord,

WHEN your lordship's elegant and ingenious paper, ON THE ANTIQUITY OF THE WOOLLEN MANUFACTURE IN IRELAND, was first read in The Royal Irish Academy, it occurred to me, that the ancient Irish Dress was a subject of more curiosity than is generally imagined. This induced me to make the present attempt. And I have now the honor to submit to your lordship the fruits of my researches.

I shall commence my enquiries at the Milesian invasion, the point at which the Irish historian and antiquary usually set out. Indeed, commencing even there, we must proceed for a while, with a cautious step; for the traces of chronology being very faint in the history of the Pagan ages of Ireland, and our path of course devious and perplexed, we are every moment in danger of going astray.

How soon after the arrival of the Milesians, the Irish threw off their Clothing of Skins I cannot venture to determine; but am inclined to think, that the dress which obtained amongst them for many centuries, and even to very late times, was introduced into this kingdom by these bold invaders (a). In support of this hypothesis I might adduce several plausible arguments; but an historian should only have to do with facts.

I shall therefore wave any attempt to shew the derivation of the Irish dress, and proceed to describe it in its earliest state from our best authorities; then follow it through all the mazes of Irish history, pausing at every stage where it suffered a change in fashion, material, or in ornament.

But our progress is stopped!—At the magic touch of Dr. Keating, an order of knights of the line of Milesius (b), armed at all points,

(a) It has been asserted by Bede and other writers, that the Cruthneans (a nation so called from the custom of painting their bodies) had intercourses, alliances, commerce and wars with the inhabitants of Ireland, at a very remote period; yet it does not appear that the Irish ever adopted the custom from which this nation derived their name.

(b) Called Curaidhe na Craoibhe ruadh, or, the knights of the Red Branch.—— O Halloran's *Introd. to Hist. of Ireland*, p. 40.

points, ſtarts up before us;—but at the frown of hiſtory, they ſink again into the ſhades of night, and only leave behind them a golden collar of exquiſite workmanſhip, now in the poſſeſſion of Mr. O'Halloran (c). The exiſtence of this collar is indiſputable, but its antiquity may be queſtioned. On ſo moot a point, I will not offer any opinion. But I cannot repreſs my ſurpriſe at the perfection of the fine arts in ſo early a period.

Having thus diſpatched thoſe airy knights, I ſhall reſume my ſubject.

The Dreſs of the ancient Iriſh conſiſted of the TRUIS or ſtrait BRACCA, the long COTA, the COCHAL, the CANABHAS, the BARRAD and the BRÔG.

The TRUIS or ſtrait BRACCA (d), was made of weft, with various colours running on it in ſtripes or diviſions. It covered the ancles, legs and thighs, riſing as high as the loins; and fitted ſo cloſe to the limbs as to diſcover every muſcle and motion of the parts which it covered.

The

(c) Ibid p. 44. Since writing the above I have learned, that Mr. O'Halloran has parted with this collar; and am informed that it exactly reſembled the collar of which Dr. CAMPBELL has given an engraving in his *Phil. Survey of the South of Ireland.* Append. Plate I. fig. 1.

(d) "The Celtic Braccæ, ſays Mr. WHITAKER, were ſo denominated from the colours running on them in ſtripes or diviſions." *Hiſt. of Mancheſt.* Vol. 1. p. 267. In vulgar Iriſh we have Bhreacàn — a Plaid.

4   AN HISTORICAL ESSAY ON

The COTA was a kind of shirt made of thin woollen stuff plaided, or of linen dyed yellow. This garment was open before and fell so far below the waist as to admit of being occasionally folded about the body, and made fast by a girdle round the loins. Of some the sleeves were short, of others long, coming down to the wrist. (*e*) Plate I. fig. 1. 3. The custom of dying this part of the dress yellow, Spencer thinks came from the east: "it was "devised (says he) in those hot countries, where saffron is very com- "mon and rife, for avoiding that evil which cometh by much sweat- "ing, and long wearing of linen." (*f*)

The

(*e*) Fig. 1. was taken from the shaft of a cross dug up in the church yard of Old Kilcullen, co. Kildare. —— Mr. WHITAKER speaking of the Cota of the Celtæ, says, " the trunk of the body was covered with a jacket which the Britons called a Co-
" ta, and we denominate a waist-coat. It was plaided, and open before, had long
" sleeves extending to the hands, and reached itself to the middle." Vol. I. p. 43. Correc.

(*f*) *View of the State of Irel.* Lord BACON assigns a more delicate, and perhaps as sound a reason for the universal use of linen shirts dyed with saffron, amongst the Irish. " The Irish (says he) wear saffroned-linen shirts, which continue long clean, and
" lengthen life; for saffron being a great binder, oily and hot, without sharpness, is very
" comfortable to the skin." *Essays*, Vol. II. p. 449, oct. ed. 1787. Lady MOIRA thinks that the Irish rather dyed their linen with a kind of lichen than with saffron, which indeed it is very probable they would have found some difficulty in obtaining in the early ages, while navigation was in its infancy; and I cannot find that the plant was indigenous, or formerly cultivated in Ireland. " The saffron-coloured linen
" Tunics, (says her Ladyship) in which Camden mentions O'Neil and his followers
" to have paid their visit to Elizabeth, were not dyed in saffron, but a kind of lichen
" that grows upon the rocks, and is prepared by the Irish as archil. I have seen of this
" dye (she continues) and it resembles in the mass, that shade of yellow which borders
" upon a dark brown." *Archæologia.* Vol. VII. p. 107.

THE DRESS OF THE IRISH.

The COCHAL or COCULA was the upper garment; a kind of long cloak, with a large hanging collar or hood of different colours (*g*). This garment only reached so low as the middle of the thigh, and was fringed with a border like shagged hair; and being brought over the shoulders, was fastened on the breast by a clasp, a buckle or DEALG FALLAINNE (or broche,) (*h*) like the garments of the high priests amongst the Jews. (*i*) Plate V. fig. 1. 2. Several of the latter instruments, some of silver, and some of pure gold, have been found in this kingdom, and are still preserved in the cabinets of the curious. (*k*) Plate II. fig. 1. 2. 3. In the field of battle the Irish wrapped the Cochal several times about the left arm, in order to make it answer the purpose of a shield. Thus the Camisolle in the days of chivalry

served

(*g*) This collar, at least in latter times consisted of many rows of shag or fringe worn partly for ornament, partly to defend the neck the better from cold; and along the edges ran a narrow fringe of the same sort of texture. WARE's *Works*, Vol. II. p. 175.

(*h*) In the eleventh century, the mantles of the Irish Kings were fastened at the neck with a golden button. See WARNER's *Hist. of Irel.* p. 424.

(*i*) *Maccab.* Chap. xiv. v. 44.

(*k*) The drawings of the Fibulæ or Broches which I have given in Plate II. fig. 1. 2. were furnished me by colonel Vallancey, and taken by him from the originals which are still extant. The original of fig. 1. is now in the Museum of Trinity College, Dublin. See also *Collect. de Reb. Hib.* Vol. 1. Plate I. *Vind. of the Anc. Hist. of Irel.* p. 459. Plate IX. But the most curious instrument of this kind that has fallen under my observation, is in the valuable collection of my friend and brother academician, Ralph Ousley, esquire, of Willsborough, Castlerea. The form is preserved in fig. 3. but neither my pen nor my pencil can give an adequate idea of the elegant gold filigreen work with which it is inlaid.

ferved amongſt the early French to weaken the force of the ſtroke of the lance (*l*).

The CANABHAS or FILLEAD (*m*) was a large looſe garment, not unlike the Cochal, and probably often worn as its ſubſtitute. Being thrown on the ſhoulders it ſpread over the whole body, and when the hood of the Cochal was drawn over the head, ſerved completely to diſguiſe the wearer. In the early ages the Canabhas was ſimply the ſkin of ſome beaſt ſlain in the chace. So Hercules was clad after having killed the Nemæan lion. We ſhall hereafter find this garment mentioned by Cambrenſis, who calls it PHALINGÆ. It was in his time a coarſe woollen cloth, ſtained black or dark purple. Such as were introduced by the Danes, were plaided or ſtriped after the manner of the Teutons. This garment appears rudely ſculptured on the croſs of St. Boyne, at Monaſter-Boice, in the county of Louth; and on a tomb in the abbey of Strade, in the county of Mayo. Plate V. fig. 1. 2. We alſo find it on a ſeal of Fedlimid, king of Connaught, given in Harris's edition of Ware's WORKS (*n*).

The Iriſh romance writers of the middle ages, give this garment to their royal perſonages, repreſenting it of a flowing length, and like the regal robes of the eaſt, of a crimſon colour (*o*). In a tranſlation of the

beautiful

(*l*) *Fabl. ou contes des xii^e et des xiii^e Siecle.* par LE GRAND. Tom. II. p. 278.

(*m*) Philleadh or Fillead, is derived from fillam, to fold, to plait or wave.

(*n*) Vol. II. p. 68. Plate I.

(*o*) Lady MOIRA informs me that the crimſon dye in Ireland is produced from a kind of moſs treated in a particular manner, which after the preparation is called Corcar, and imparts a crimſon colour.

beautiful Irish romance of THE DEATH OF CUCHOLINN (*p*), now before me, it is related, that " CUCHOLINN rose up suddenly, and as he " was rising up, part of his mantle got under his left foot, and ob- " liged him to sit down against his will: he was ashamed and vexed " at this accident, and rose up again in some confusion, when the gol- " den bodkin in his mantle flew out, and falling downwards pierced " his foot through to the ground." On this circumstance a learned correspondent observes with equal good sense and ingenuity, " that there was evidently a grace annexed in those days, to a person's wear- ing that Robe without appearing encumbered by it; since the shame and vexation that CUCHOLINN is made to feel from en- tangling his foot in his Mantle, is not expressed as the result of superstition."

The BARRAD was a conical Cap, not unlike the cap worn at pre- sent by our grenadiers, but with this difference, that the cone of the Barrad usually hung behind. " Ils étoient Coëffés d'un bonnet (says l'Abbé Ma-Geoghegan) fait de la même étoffe que leur habit, & élevé en pointe." (*q*) On the figure of a bard lately discovered in the ruins of Old Kilcullen, there appears one of these caps. Plate. I. fig. 4. (*r*). So partial were the Irish to the Barrad that they thought

it

(*p*) Oiohe Chonchulluin.

(*q*) *Hist. d' Irlande*, Tom. 1. p. 90.

(*r*) Vide *Hist. Mem. of the Irish Bards*, p. 14. It appears also on the figure of a Bag-piper in the illumination of a copy of KEATING's *Hist. of Irel.* in the original Irish, now in the possession of Dr. Archer, which was executed by William Lynch in 1698.

A Barrad,

it would fit an Angel; accordingly we find it on the head of two Angels in an ancient piece of sculpture lately dug up in the churchyard of St. Peter's, Drogheda. The Scotch Bonnet was also formerly in use in this country. Plate I. fig. 6. And for several ages many of the inhabitants of Connaught wore no other covering on the head than the hood of the Cochula, fastened under the chin by means either of a string or clasp; or a CAILLEACH or KERCHER flowing from the crown of the head down on the shoulders. Of the latter garment Mr. Beauford favoured me with delineations, which he accompanied with the following description. "The old Irish Ker-
"cher, (says he) which I have represented in (Plate I.) fig. 2. was
"denominated a Callach or Cailleach, and was worn equally by both
"sexes; but usually by the men as in (Plate I.) fig. 1. and made of
"the skin of a beast. This Cap is represented on stone-crosses at
"Clonmacnoise, and at Old Kilcullen. It was worn in the western
"isles of Scotland during the last century."

But

A Barrad, answering exactly the description of our historians, was seen a few years since, on one Hugh Dungan, a yeoman of the county of Kilkenny, who always affected the antient Irish Dress, and who on that account was the gaze of the vulgar: my informant has often seen him followed by troops of wondering boys.

It has been suggested to me by an ingenious friend, that in the early ages the Irish Cap, like that of the Egyptians, might have been one of the marks of distinction, and that it probably varied its form or ornaments accordingly. — This friend also directed my notice to the engraving of a Druidic Sacrifice found on a rock near the ruins of Babair, in which the Priests wear Caps resembling the Irish Barrad. See *Montfaucon's Antiq.* Vol. II. *Supp.* b. 7. cap. 1.

THE DRESS OF THE IRISH.

But it was in adorning the heads of their Druids that the ancient Irish displayed their taste and brought to light the hidden wealth of their country. While those artful Priests were employed in sacrifices and other ceremonies, they wore, behind an oak-leafed crown, a Golden Crescent with buttons at the extremities, through which a string was drawn that served to fasten it behind. Plate, III. fig. 4. Several of these Crescents have been found in our bogs. In general the blank parts appear to have been radiated with a tool, but Colonel Vallancey saw one, that instead of being tooled, was plaited like a lady's fan *(s)*.

While we have the Druids before us, let us not pass by their Dress unnoticed. This we are told was uniformly and universally a white garment, emblematic of the affected purity of their mind. And in order to render their appearance more venerable and more imposing, they encouraged their beards to flow on their breast. Thus a modern poet describes one of this order of men:

> His seemly beard, to grace his form bestow'd,
> Descending decent, on his bosom flow'd:
> His robe of purest white, though rudely join'd
> Yet shew'd an emblem of the purest mind;
> Stern virtue, beaming on his eye, controul'd
> Each wayward purpose, and o'eraw'd the bold *(t)*.

Mention

(s) Collect. de Reb. Hib. No. XIII. p. 70, 71.
(t) Fane of the Druids, p. 3.

Mention of the Dress of our Druids, reminds me of that of our Bards; but having treated of that subject elsewhere *(u)*, I shall only observe, from a recent publication, that amongst the early Irish the mantle of the Ollamhain was denominated SUADH *(v)*.

It is justly observed by an humorous author, that the Shoe, in one form or another, is nearly as antient as the foot. We may therefore, venture to give the BROG or BROGUE, to the early Irish. "This, (says Harris,) in ancient times, was made of the dried skins of beasts, but afterwards of raw half tanned leather, as at the present day, and fastened to the foot by means of a latchet or thong, made of the same sort of skin *(w)*." In form the Brôg differed little from the Sandal, each consisting chiefly of a single sole, and level from toe to heel. The ancient Irish also wore
a kind

(u) Hist. Mem. of Irish Bards.

(v) Vind. of Anc. Hist. of Irel. p. 206.

(w) WARE's *Works*, Vol. II. p. 178. The Brogue did not escape the observation of Shakespear, on which, with great propriety, he bestows the epithet "clouted"; I say with propriety, for to clout means to cover or patch, and according to Mr. Whitaker, "the " shoes of the Celts must have been equally party-coloured as the rest of their Dress, " as they were equally with the Trowsers denominated Brac or Brag, and are still " denominated Brôg." Vol. I. p. 228. In the celebrated ballad of *Edward* IV. *and the Tanner of Tamworth*, the Tanner tells the King, that

" If ever thou comest to merry Tamworth,
Neates leather shall *clout* thy shoen."

THE DRESS OF THE IRISH.

a kind of Buſkin or ſhort Boot, anſwering to the Britiſh Butis, the Scotch Mullion *(x)*, and the Roman Perones *(y)*. One of theſe was found not long ſince in a bog in the Queen's County, and is in the poſſeſſion of a gentleman who has favoured me with the following deſcription of it. " It is made of raw ſkin with the hair turned out-
" wards, is open before, but was intended, when on the leg, to be
" laced in front with thongs of leather. The ſole appears never to have
" been thicker than the upper part *(z)*."

Amongſt the early Iriſh, the BEARD was cheriſhed with as much ſolicitude, as formerly amongſt the Orientals *(a)*. Nor did they reſtrain the growth of the hair on the head; but throwing it back from the forehead, allowed it to flow about the neck, calling thoſe ſuſpended locks COLUNS or GLIBBS, and taking an honeſt pride in them. *(b)* On the capital of a pillar found amidſt the ruins of Glendaloch

in

(x) CAMDEN's *Brit.* apud GIBSON, Introd. p. 118. In Scotland the Buſkin was called alſo Cockers or Cutikens. Thus in an old ballad, ——

" His Cockers were of Cordievin."

(y) KENNET's *Antiq. of Rome,* p. 323.

(z) This anſwers Mr. WHITAKER's deſcription of the ancient Buſkin of the Iriſh and Highlanders. Vol. 1. p. 45. Correct.

(a) Vide *An Hiſt. Eſſay on Beards,* p. 18. a work of humour and learning. See alſo *A Code of Gentoo Laws,* ch. 17.

(b) In the tranſlation of the Iriſh and Erſe tales publiſhed ſome years ſince, under the general title of OSSIAN's *Poems,* we find frequent alluſions to the Glibb, equally worn by both nations.

in the county of Wicklow, is exhibited a youthful Head with the genuine Irish Glibb. Plate. I. fig. 5. The statute of Hen. VIII. which obliged the Irish to cut off their Coluns, gave occasion to a song, of which the air is now universally admired *(c)*.

Amongst the ornaments which formerly adorned the fair daughters of this isle, the BODKIN is peculiarly deserving our notice. Whence the Irish derived this implement, I might conjecture, but cannot determine. Altho' I have pursued it with an eager enquiry, I have not been able to trace it beyond the foundation of the celebrated palace of Eamania. The design of this palace (according to our old chroniclers) was sketched on a bed of sand by the Empress Macha, with her Bodkin. If this tradition be founded in reality, Bodkins must have been worn by the Irish Ladies several centuries before the Christian Æra. But I should be contented to give them a less remote, provided I could assign them a more certain antiquity. If the word Aiccde in the Brehon laws will admit of being translated a Bodkin, we may infer their use in Ireland about the commencement of the Christian Æra: for in a code of sumptuary laws of the second century, we find frequent mention of the Aiccde (*d*). But I am rather inclined to consider the Aiccde as a kind of Broche from the circumstance of its marking the rank of the wearer by its value, as was formerly the case amongst the Highlanders, whose frequent intercourse with the Irish, occasion-

ed

(c) Vide *Hist. Mem. of Irish Bards*, p. 134

(d) *Collect. de Reb. Hib.* Vol. 1.

ed a striking similarity in the customs and manners of both people.

This instrument was known in Ireland under several names, viz; COITIT, DEALG, MEANNADH. Its uses were two-fold: it was equally worn in the breast and head. The custom of wearing the Bodkin in the breast, is alluded to in the following passage of an old Irish M. S. romance, called, THE INTERVIEW BETWEEN FION MA CUBHALL AND CANNAN *(e)*.——"Cannan, when he said this, was "seated at the table; on his right hand sat his wife, and upon his left "his beautiful daughter Findalve, so exceedingly fair, that the snow "driven by the winter storm surpassed not her fairness, and her "cheeks were the colour of the blood of a young calf. Her hair "hung in curling ringlets, and her teeth were like pearls. A spacious "veil hung from her lovely head down on her delicate body, and "the veil was bound by a *Golden Bodkin*."

Such Bodkins as were worn in the head, were termed DEALG-FUILT. Even at this day the female peasants in the interior parts of this kingdom, like the women of the same class in Spain and Turkey, collect their hair at top, and *(f)* twisting it several times, make it fast with a Bodkin.

Besides

(e) Comhbháil eadar Fhionn mhac Cumhaill, agus Conán. This Romance is in the collection of the Countess of MOIRA.

(f) This was also the custom of the ancient Germans. "Insigne gentis, obliquare crinem." TACIT. And MARTIAL, "Crinibus in nodum tortis venere Sicambri."

Besides those uses, the Bodkin had another: it was sometimes made to answer the purpose of a Needle. Hence its name of MEANNADH-FUAGHALA. To be so employed it must have had an eye. It is in a Bodkin of this kind that Pope's Ariel threatens to imprison such of his Sylphs as are careless of their charge.

"Or plung'd in lakes of bitter washes lie,
Or wedg'd whole ages in a Bodkin's Eye." *(g)*

Whether or not the Irish Ladies, like those of the neighbouring nations *(h)*, employed their Bodkins as weapons offensive and defensive, neither tradition nor history informs us. But such of those implements as I have seen, certainly seemed as capable of making a man's *quietus*, as that with which Julius Cæsar is said to have been killed *(i)*, or that with which Simekin in the REVES TALE protected the honour of his wife *(k)*.

But perhaps we should not confine our Bodkin to the toilet of the fair. However I shall let it remain there until I am properly authorised either to give it a place in the breast, or to bury its body in the hair of the ancient heroes of this Isle. According to the ingenious Mr. Whitaker, Bodkins constituted a part of the ornamental Dress of

(g) Rape of the Lock. Cant. II.
(h) See PERCEY's *Reliq.* Vol. II. p. 343.
(i) STOWE's *Chron.* ed. 1614. RANDOLPH's *Muse's Looking-Glass.*
(k) TYRWHITT's *Chaucer,* Vol. I. p. 154.

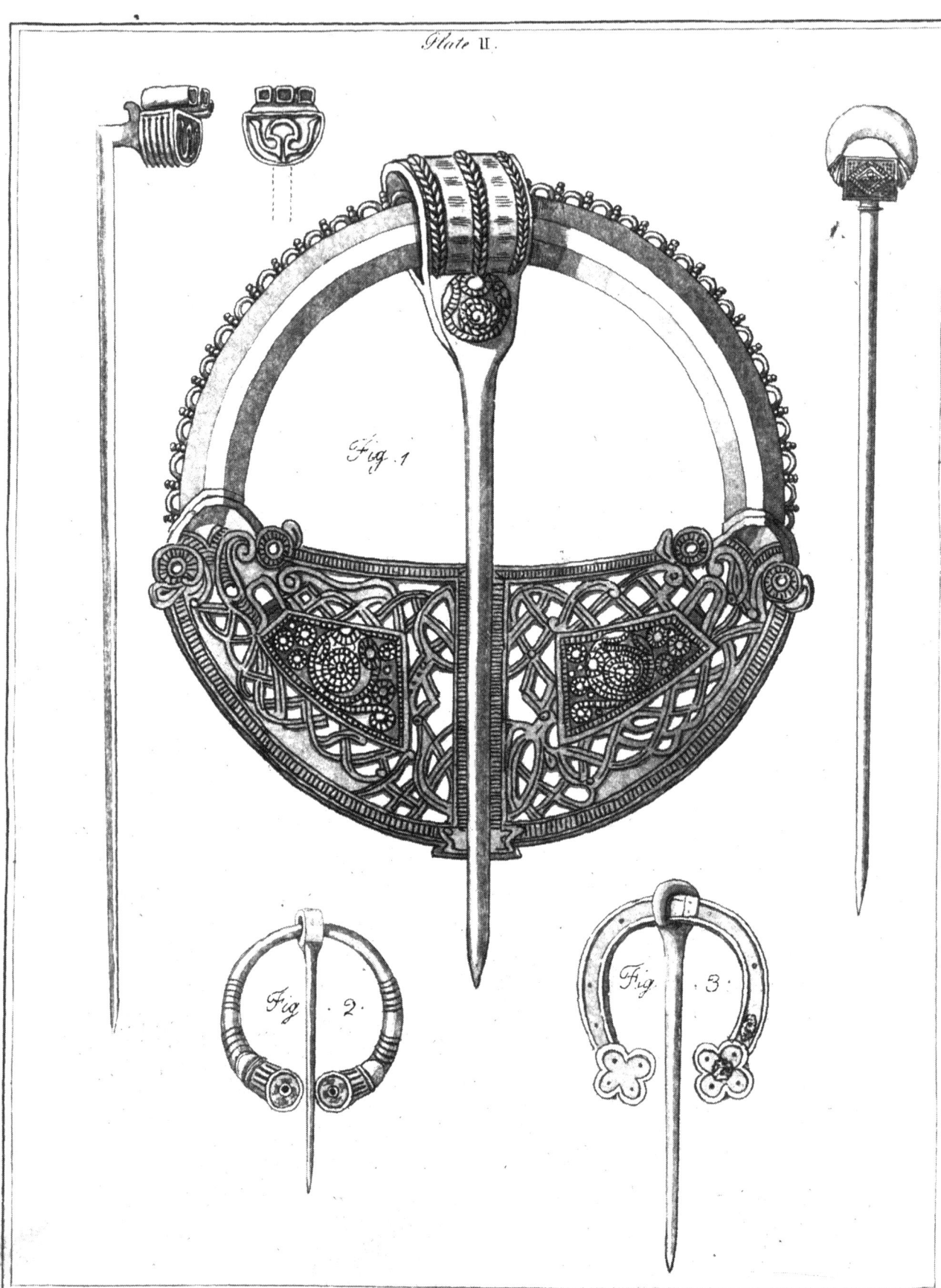

THE DRESS OF THE IRISH.

of the early British kings. This he afferts on the authority of Coins *(l)*. And from the works of fome of the old English Dramatifts it appears, that Bodkins were worn by Englifhmen during the middle ages *(m)*.

It now remains to exhibit a few of thofe implements found in different parts of this kingdom.

Plate II. fig. 4. 5. are made of brafs. They are both in the Mufeum of Trinity College. Dublin. Plate V. fig. 3. was found in the county of Limerick, 1775. It is made of brafs, weighs 3 oz. and is 5½ inches long. This inftrument is in the poffeffion of Ralph Oufley, Efq; of Willfboro' near Caftlerea,— as is fig. 4, of brafs alfo, which was found at Knockglafs, in the county of Rofcommon, in July, 1782. It weighs 2¼ oz. has a fliding ring, and is 8 inches long. Fig. 5. is made of filver. It is a large Pin, one third of the length of which is neatly fluted like a miniature column. It is now in the poffeffion of the Countefs of Granard.

Having thus defined and defcribed with all the accuracy in my power, the feveral articles of the ancient Irifh Drefs, I fhall now commence my promifed hiftorical purfuit, occafionally glancing, as I proceed, at the Habits of our fellow fubjects in Great Britain.

The

(l) Hift. of Manch. Vol. II.

(m) RANDOLPH, BEAUMONT and FLETCHER, SHAKESPEAR.

The firſt innovation in the Iriſh Dreſs, after the Mileſian invaſion, took place (if our annals are to be credited) in the reign of Tighernmas A. M. 2815. This prince, we are told, ordained a ſumptuary law called Ilbreachta, † according to which the different claſſes of the people were to be diſtinguiſhed by the number of colours in their garments—thus: The Peaſantry and Soldiers were to wear garments of one colour; — military Officers and private Gentlemen, of two; — Commanders of battalions, of three; Beatachs, Buighnibbs, or Keepers of houſes of hoſpitality, of four; the principal Nobility and Knights, of five; the Ollamhs or dignified Bards, of ſix; and the Kings and Princes of the blood, of ſeven *(n)*. At this diſtant period a further enquiry concerning thoſe diſcriminating garments, would be attended with little ſucceſs. But I muſt not omit to obſerve, that according to The Liber Lecanus, * this prince introduced the dying of cloth with purple, blue and green; an art cultivated in the

---

(†) Ilbꞃeachta.

(n) O'Conor, O'Halloran, Mac Curtin, Grat. Lucius, Ma-Geoghegan. This variety of colours in the garments of the Iriſh continued to very late times. Cambrensis alludes to it in *Top. Hib.* diſt. 3. c. 10. and it is thus particularly deſcribed by Harris: " The Iriſh Mantles (ſays he) with the fringed or " ſhagged border ſewed down the edges of it, was not always made of Frize, or " ſuch coarſe materials, which was the Dreſs of the lower ſort of people; but accord- " ing to the rank or quality of the wearer was ſometimes made of the fineſt cloth, " bordered with ſilken or fine woollen fringe, and of ſcarlet and other various co- " lours." Ware's *Works*, Vol. II. p. 175. If I thought it would be admitted, I would adduce poetical authority to ſhew, that the higher claſſes of the early Iriſh wore garments interwoven with threads of gold.

* Leabhaꞃ Leacán.

THE DRESS OF THE IRISH.

the remoteſt ages in Phœnicia, Egypt, India, and the land of Canaan. (o)

Amongſt the inſtitutes of that wiſe prince Olamh Fodhla, I cannot find any regulation reſpecting Dreſs; but it ſhould ſeem from the deſcriptions which remain of the triennial meetings at Tara, in his reign, that his capacious hall, on thoſe occaſions glittered, with all the gaudy trappings of ancient Chivalry. ——

> Stately the feaſt, and high the cheer:
> Girt with many an armed peer.

But I ſhall not detain your Lordſhip any longer in this fairy land of fable; for ſuch we muſt conſider the Pagan ages of Ireland, till their hiſtory, as handed down to us, has ſtood the teſt of more critical enquiry.

The veil which time had drawn over the Iriſh Dreſs, from the reign of Tighernmas to the commencement of the Chriſtian Æra, was at length removed

---

(o) The dye-ſtuffs which, according to Sir WILLIAM PETTY, were in uſe amongſt the Iriſh in 1672 for dying their linen and woollen cloth, they probably owed their knowledge of to their early anceſtors; for they ſeem to have been the ſuggeſtions of nature in the infancy of ſociety. "Madder, Allum, and Indigo (ſays my author) are "imported, but the other dying ſtuffs they find nearer home; a certain mud taken "out of the bogs ſerving them for copperas, the rind of ſeveral trees, and ſaw-duſt, "for galls; as for wild and green weeds, they find enough, as alſo of Rhamnus ber- "ries." *The Polit. Anat. of Irel.* p. 81.

removed by Benin, the difciple and fucceffor of St. Patrick. In THE BOOK OF GLENDALOGH (*p*), attributed to this writer, in which are inferted, from THE BOOK OF RIGHTS (*q*), the ancient laws of fubfidies, tributes and regal rights, we find mention of fcarlet filk Cloaks, with gold clafps and rich embroidery; Coats of Mail; Shields of curious workmanfhip; Swords richly mounted; gold-hilted Swords, (*r*) and horfes magnificently accoutred, particularly with golden bitted Bridles. Allowing that all this finery was exotic, the medium through which it paffed into this country, is difcoverable in the following paffages of Tacitus. Speaking of Ireland he fays, " Solum cœlumque et ingenia cultufque " hominum haud multum a Britanniâ differunt: melius aditus portufque " per commercia & negotiatores cogniti." (*s*) " In foil and climate, as " alfo in the temper and manners of the natives, it varies little from Britain: Its ports and landings are better known, through the frequency " of commerce and merchants."

Under the reign of Mogha Nuadhad, who was killed at the battle of Maglean in the King's County, A. D. 192, a code of fumptuary laws was

(*p*) Leabhar Glinndaloch.

(*q*) Leabhar na Cceart. This book, Dr. RAYMOND fays, is the oldeft book of hiftory extant, next to the Greek and Roman. *Introd. to Hift. of Irel.*

(*r*) Some years fince there were found in the bog of Cullen, in the county of Tipperary, fome gorgets of gold, and gold-headed fwords, feemingly of high antiquity. O'HALLORAN's *Introd. to Hift. of Irel.* p. 147. And about twenty years ago, feveral corfelets of pure gold were difcovered on the lands of Clonties, in the county of Kerry. SMITH's *Hift. of Kerry*, p. 186-7.

(*s*) *Jul. Agricol. Vita.*

THE DRESS OF THE IRISH.

was enacted, from which I shall make a few extracts in the tranflation of my learned friend, colonel Vallancey: (*t*)

" The lawful value of a filver Bodkin, (*u*) is by cuftom to be paid in cumals of heifers."

" The lawful value of a filver Bodkin to an Oc-airech is three heifers."

" The lawful value of a filver Bodkin to a Bo-airich is five heifers."

" The lawful value of a filver Bodkin to every Airech (or Noble) up to an Airech-forgill is ten heifers."

" The lawful value of a filver Bodkin to an Airech-Forgill of the loweft rank, is fifteen heifers."

" The lawful value of a filver Bodkin to a King, or Profeffor, (a Bard or Ollamh) is thirty heifers, if the fame be made of refined filver."

" The

(*t*) The original, together with the tranflation of this code of laws, may be found in *Collec. de Reb. Hib.* No. iv.

(*u*) The Bodkin mentioned in thofe laws was, I prefume, of the nature of the Broches already delineated and defcribed. See Plate II. fig. 1. 2. 3.

" The lawful price of fervants cloaths is alike to all degrees of Airech-feibhes, and feven heifers is the price of each fervants cloathing."

" The lawful price of cloaths for holydays is alike to all Airech-febes, and they are to pay for the fame in three gales."

" The lawful price of the cloathing of a King's fervant is equal to that of the holyday cloathing of an Airech-febe."

" The lawful price of a King's holyday cloathing, out of gratitude and love to his perfon, fhall be valued at three common fuits, to be paid at three gales."

" The lawful value of cloathing to a Poetefs, or to the wife of a Bard, according to the old law. If he be of long ftanding in the tribe, it is proper he fhould be made free. Three milch cows is the value of a free Poet's cloathing, and of his wife's: it is the fame from the chief Bard of a Flaith (petty prince) to the Ollamh or Poet laureat; and the value of their wive's cloathing is the fame."

" The lawful price of the cloathing of an Ollamh or Poet laureat, and of the Anra or fecond Poet, is five milch cows."

" The value of Needle-Work, according to the old law. A young bullock or fteer, is the payment for a mantle wrought with the needle, or an heifer is equal payment."

" The value of Embroidery, according to the old law: for work of this kind properly done and completely finifhed, the reward is an

ounce

THE DRESS OF THE IRISH.

ounce of filver: more is to be paid for extraordinary work in proportion." (*v*)

" The lawful price of a Queen's cloathing, if fhe brought a regal dowry, is fix cows; but if fhe brought no dowry the payment to be made in proportion to the value of the cloathing." (*w*)

On thofe laws I will take leave to obferve, that the fpirit of the ILBREACHTA of Tighernmas, which directed the diftinction of the claffes of the people by means of their garments, feems to have been maintained through feveral Pagan ages; and that therefore an afperfion of barbarifm has been unjuftly thrown on the heathen times of Ireland: for obedience to the laws, it muft be allowed, is incompatible with a ftate of actual barbarifm, though it may not argue a ftate of elegant refinement.

From thefe laws alfo it appears, that filver was at this time, and probably much earlier, abounding in Ireland (*x*), and that the people were

no

(*v*) An old commentator on this law fays, " divers colours on fcarlet filk is to be paid for according to its merit."

(*w*) On this law alfo we find a comment by an old fcholiaft. "This cloathing may confift of body cloaths, a golden head-drefs in form of a crown, a golden veil or a filver chain for the neck, provided the chain does not weigh more than 3 ounces: the value of the chain lefs than 3 ounces, is only three cows."

(*x*) It fhould feem that this ifland teemed with filver. For as well as in the laws recited, we find an act was ordained in 35 Hen. VI. that merchants ftrangers fhall pay forty pence

no ſtrangers to the mechanic arts, or at leaſt had taſte and juſtice enough to ſet a due value on their productions—nay, even on the productions of the needle.

Nor was the ſplendour of thoſe days confined to the arms and garments of the Iriſh; we find golden crowns glittering on the heads of their princes (*y*). According to O'Flagherty, the golden Aſion (or crown) of Queen Caſhire the Great, was ſtolen A. D. 174, at the convention of Tara (*z*). Several golden crowns of exquiſite workmanſhip, and evidently anterior to the chriſtian Æra, have been found in this kingdom; one of which, that was dug out of a bog in the county of Tipperary in 1692, is ſuppoſed to be ſtill extant in France (*a*). Plate III. fig. 5. From ſome rude paintings in freſco in the Abbey of Knockmoy in the county of Galway, the form of the Iriſh crown in the twelfth century may be determined (*b*). Plate III. fig. 1. 2. 3. And its form at other periods is ſtill preſerved on ſepulchral monuments

---

pence cuſtom for every pound of ſilver that they carry out of Ireland; and lord Strafford in one of his letters from Dublin to his royal maſter ſays, " with this I ſend an ingot of ſilver, of 300 oz." Vol. I. p. 174.

(*y*) We are told by HUGH WARD that, " all the Kings of Ireland in battle, and on other publick ſolemnities, appeared crowned with a diadem." *Vita Rumoldi.* p. 170. It is well known that Brien Boroimhe, the monarch of Ireland, who fell by the hands of the Danes in the memorable battle of Ciontarf (A. D. 1014), was diſcovered by means of the royal crown on his head.

(*z*) *Ogygia.* p. 46.

(*a*) *Collect. de Reb. Hib.* Vol. IV. p. 39. WARE's *Works*, Vol. II.

(*b*) This abbey was founded in the year 1189, ARCHDALL.

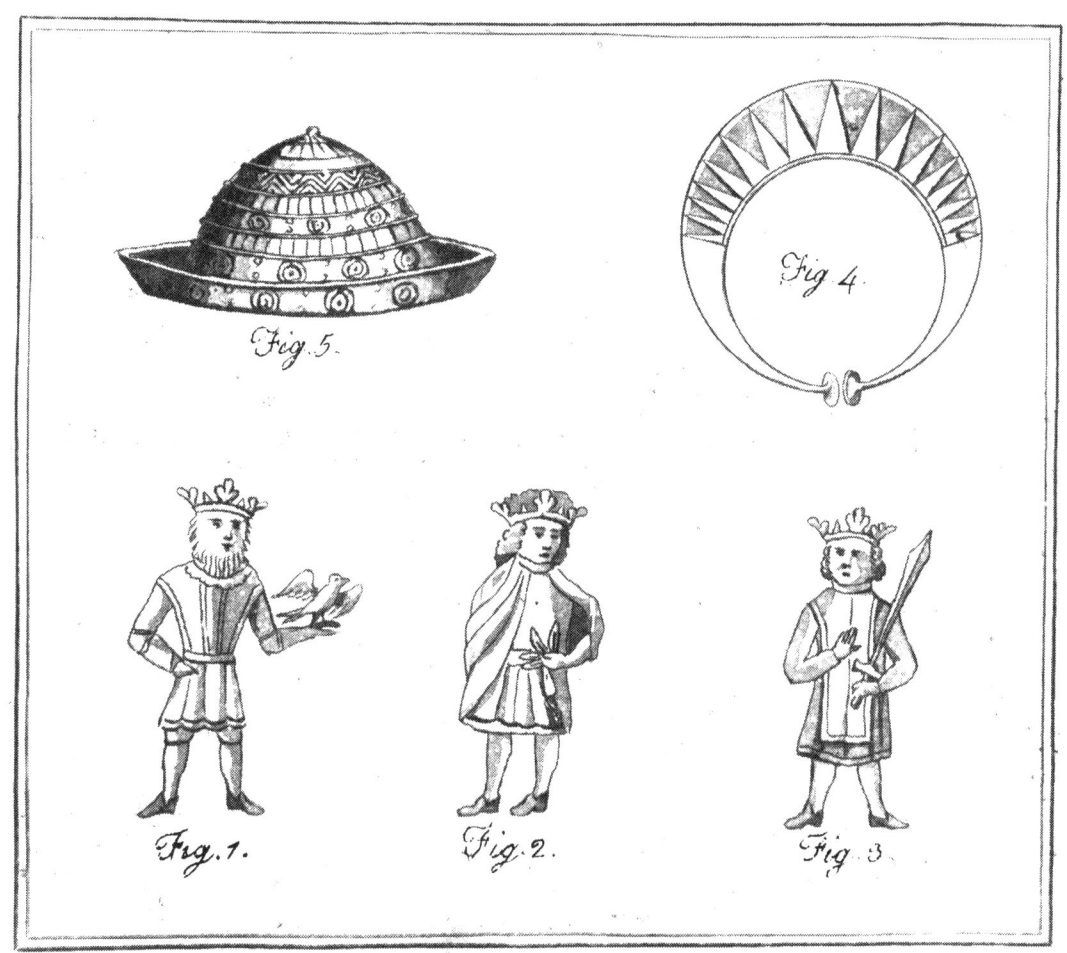

Plate 3.

monuments in different parts of the kingdom. Plate V. fig. 1. 2. (*c*)

With Christianity undoubtedly was introduced an innovation in the habits of those who took up the cross. But as this innovation was confined to ecclesiasticks, and operated agreeably to the rules of the several religious orders, all of which were originally instituted in other countries, it does not properly come within my plan. For the same reason I shall omit all mention of the Armour of the military religious orders. I shall therefore pass by the church, and proceed to the next stage in the national dress of the Irish.

According to Nennius, a British writer of the ninth century, the Irish princes in his time, hung pearls behind their ears (*d*). This ridiculous fashion was adopted by the dignified clergy in a later period. In the ruins of the church of the abbey of Duleek, in the county of Meath, there is a monumental figure of one of the Abbots, with a string of pearls, hanging behind each ear.

The tenth century was an age of great splendour. This we learn from the will of Cormac, King of Munster, and bishop of Cashel, which I shall give in the translation of doctor Warner, referring your lordship for

(*c*) Besides the figures to which I refer, there are drawings of several other regal sepulchral figures in my possession, each with a crown on its head.

(*d*) *De mirab. Hibern.* Pearls once abounded, and are still found in this country: Lady MOIRA saw some that were taken out of the river Ban. In the eleventh century the Irish pearls were in such high repute, that Gilbert bishop of Limerick, considered a present of them as the most acceptable gift he could offer Anselm, bishop of Canterbury, to whom it is probable he was indebted for his church preferments. Vide HARRIS's ed. of WARE's *Works*, Vol. II. p. 172.

for the original to Keating's HISTORY OF IRELAND. Thus his legacies are enumerated: " An ounce of gold, an ounce of silver, his horse
" and furniture, to Ardfinnan; a gold and silver chalice and vestment
" of silk, to Lismore; a gold and silver chalice, four ounces of gold and
" five of silver, to Cashel; three ounces of gold and a mass book, to
" Emly; an ounce of gold and an ounce of silver, to Glendaloch; a
" horse and furniture, an ounce of gold and an embroidered vestment,
" to Kildare; three ounces of gold, to Iniscashy; three ounces of gold,
" an embroidered vestment, and his blessing, to Mountgarret; and four
" and twenty ounces of gold and silver, to Armagh; besides legacies, to
" his friends, amongst which were a golden chain and a royal robe em-
" broidered with gold and jewels." (*e*)

As the authenticity of his will has not been questioned, it may be safely presumed, that Silk, by being enumerated amongst Cormac's bequests, was in use in Ireland before it reached England; for the learned Mr. Gough, who was certainly well informed on the subject, is of opinion that silk was not introduced into England till the reign of Henry II. (*f*)

Soon after the death of Cormac arose Murkertagh, a prince who wielded the sword with as much ability as Cormac had wielded the pen.

(*e*) *Hist. of Irel.* Vol. II. It is observed by Lord LYTTLETON on this will, that " the
" gold which the princes of Ireland then possessed, was the produce of their commerce
" with the Ostmen inhabiting their principal cities, who purchased with it their cattle,
" and other commodities which their country afforded." *Life of Henry* II. Vol. IV.
p. 289.

(*f*) *Sepulch. Mon. of Great Brit.* Vol. I.

THE DRESS OF THE IRISH.

This prince, more folicitous to protect than adorn the perfons of his fubjects, invented leathern coverings or jackets, impenetrable to the arrows and javelins of the enemy. To this invention he owed the afcititious name of Muirkertach na Geochall Croceann (*g*).

The ufe of Golden Collars, or Gorgets, in the next age, is fhewn by the following paffage in that valuable inedited Irifh manufcript, THE ANNALS OF INNISFALLEN:

1004. "Sluagh le Brian go bfeapaibh Eineann uime, go Cineal Eogain, agus "go holltaibh, gup chumgioh gialla Mihe; go mbaoap aichche Attailtean, "go noeachaoap go Sliabh Fuaio, agus ar sin go hApomhacha, go pabhaoap "reachtmhuin ann: go bhfagaibh Brian fail óip ionna paibh fichche unga oo "ohiepc aip altóip mhóip Apoamhacha. Oo chuaioh Brian ar sin go paith mhóip "Mhuighe Line, go ttug geille Ohail Nap uiohe leis. King Brian marched at "the head of a powerful army of the men of Ireland into Kineal "Eogain, (now Tyrone), and in his way took hoftages from "Meath, remained a night at Talteann, and from thence marched "by Sliabh-Fuad to Ardmagh, where he remained with his army an en- "tire week, and at his departure left a *Golden Collar*, weighing twenty "ounces, as an offering, on the great altar. He marched from thence to "the great fort or palace of Moylinny, and took hoftages from Dalnary." What has been the fate of this rich donation, hiftory does not inform us; but it is well known that feveral golden collars have been found in this kingdom, which antiquaries affign to the period now under confideration,

(g) O'CONOR's *Differt. on the Hift. of Irel.* p. 249.

fideration, and for which I am inclined to think that the Irish were indebted to the Danes. In a skirmish between a party of the Danes, and Donald IV. in the year 980, we find Malachy, the heir to the throne, stripping a golden collar from the neck of one of their champions (*h*). Fusion, so fatal to relics of antiquity, has deprived us of many of these collars; some, however, have escaped, and, at this hour, not only enrich the cabinets of virtuosi (*i*), but live in works that will be read and admired when this essay, and its author shall be forgotten. See COLLECT. DE REB. HIBERN. Vol. IV. Plate I. PHILOSOPH. SURVEY OF THE SOUTH OF IRELAND. Append. Plate I. fig. 1.

It is matter of much regret, that no description has been preserved of the regal robe of so wealthy and powerful a monarch as Brian; but it may be presumed it resembled that with which he presented Malmorda, the King of Leinster. This, according to doctor Warner, was a rich silk Mantle, embroidered with gold and silver, fringed with lace of great value, and fastened at the neck with a golden button (*k*).

About

(*h*) WARNER, p. 404.

(*i*) While speaking of collars we must not forget the miraculous collar or breast-plate of Moran, which, according to the credulous Dr. KEATING, would close round the neck of the wearer, if he attempted to pronounce a false sentence, and continue to squeeze him till he had given the proper verdict. Two collars of gold found in our bogs, both supposed to have been worn, like Moran's, by Irish pagan judges, but not endued with the same powers, are still extant. One of these (weighing 10wts. 10grs.) which was found twelve feet deep in a turf bog in the county of Limerick, is now in the possession of Mrs. Bury of Granby-row, Dublin.

(*k*) Hist. of Irel. p. 424.

THE DRESS OF THE IRISH.

About this time, a daring attempt was meditated by Æd, an erudite monk, to introduce the Tonsure amongst the young females committed to his tuition. Warned by their Sylphs, the ladies arose in defence of their hair, and poor Æd, to escape the fate of Orpheus, was obliged to seek for safety in exile (*l*).

It should seem that the Irish, as it were in a fit of despair, put off all their finery on the approach of the English; for Cambrensis, an eye witness, thus describes their Dress.—" Laneis enim tenuiter utuntur & his " omnibus ferme nigris, (quia terræ istius oves nigræ sunt,) & barbaro ri- " tu compositis" (*m*). He then enters into a more minute description of their Dress. " Caputiis namque modicis assueti sunt & arctis, trans " humeros deorsum, cubito tenus protensis (*n*), variifque colorum gene- " ribus

---

(*l*) WARE's *Works*, Vol. II. p. 240. Æd's banishment happened A. D. 1053.

(*m*) GRAT. LUCIUS takes much pains to prove, that this assertion of Cambrensis is without foundation. SPEED, a writer of simplicity and fidelity observes, " their sheep " (speaking of the Irish) are many, but bear not the best wool, which twice are shorne " within one year. Of these they make mantles, caddowes and coverlets, vented from " thence into fourine countries." *Theat. of the Emp. of Great Brit.* At this day the peasantry of Connaught and Munster (where the primitive customs and manners still prevail) are clad agreeably to the description of Cambrensis and Speed. This I assert from observation, having, not long since, travelled through those provinces.

(*n*) From this description of the Caputiæ it appears, that they bore an exact resemblance to the Phrygian cap which is worn by the bagpiper in MACCARI's *Diss. sopr' un Suonator di Cornamusa.* Vide App. No. 4. to *Hist. Mem. of Irish Bards.* We also find a Cappucio on Spenser's Doubt. *Fairy Queen.* Book 3. cant. 12. st. 10.

"ribus panni colorumque plerumque confutis: fub quibus phalingis (o) "laneis quoque palliorum vice utuntur, feu braccis caligatis feu caligis "braccatis, & his plerumque colore fucatis. Item fellis equitando "non utuntur, non ocreis, non calcaribus: virgâ tantum, quam manu "geftant, in fuperiori parte camerata, tam equos excitant, quam ad cur- "fus invitant." He proceeds, "frenis quidem utuntur, tam chami "quam freni vice fungentibus, quibus & equi femper herbis "affueti, ad pabula nequaquam impediuntur." (p) "The Irifh "wear thin woollen cloaths, moftly black, becaufe the fheep of Ireland "are in general of that colour. The drefs itfelf is of a barbarous "fafhion.—They wear light Cappuces, which fpread over their fhoul- "ders and reach down to the elbow. Thefe upper coverings are made of "fabrics of different textures, with other fabrics of divers colours ftitch- "ed on them in ftripes. Under thefe, they wear woollen Filleadth or "Fallings, inftead of the Pallium, befides large loofe breeches or trowfers, "and thefe, for the moft part, dyed. In riding they ufe no faddles, nor "do they wear boots or fpurs; carrying only a fwitch rounded at the "upper end, as well to excite their horfes to mend their pace, as to fet "forward in full fpeed. They ufe indeed bridles and bits, but fo contriv- "ed as not to hinder the horfes of their pafture, in a land where thefe "animals only feed on green grafs."

The

(o) "Phalingis laneis, a kind of coarfe cloth, anfwering to the Falding, in which Chau- "cer clothes his Shipman." TYRWHITT. Fallin—in Irifh. LLHUYD.

(p) *Top. Hib. Dift.* III. Cap. 10.

Plate 4.

THE DRESS OF THE IRISH.

The next description of the Irish dress, in the order of chronology, is supplied us by a Danish annalist. In the ANTIQUITATES CELTO-SCANDICÆ lately published by the learned Dr. Johnstone, we find under the year 1129, the Dress of Heraldus Gellius, who, " hibernico fere " utebatur amictu," thus described: " venit ille, et hoc quidem modo vesti-" tus; interulam braccasque (talares,) ligulis sub plantis constrictis, et " breve pallium indutus, capite pilium hibernicum, hastile autem manu " gestabat."

In order to illustrate in some degree this description of the Danish annalist, Sculpture kindly advances with a monument of the military dress of our countrymen in the period under consideration. This monument, is the tomb of O'Conor, at Roscommon, which was erected A. D. 1292,—and which your lordship will find faithfully delineated in Plate IV. as it appeared in the present year (1787).

With regard to the Dresses of the Irish Princes from whom King John received homage and oaths of fealty, we are only informed, that " they laid aside their Girdles, their Skeans *(q)* and their Caps, when they were

preparing

(q) The Irish Skean (or Scian) answered to the English Anelace, and the knights Misericorde of the middle ages; and was also worn as an ornament. We find anelaces hanging to the girdles of the Frankeleen, and the five mechanics of Chaucer. Prol. to *Cant. Tales.* v. 370. 375. It is worthy of observation, that the anelace which hangs from a button on the breast of Chaucer in his portrait given amongst the illustrious heads, closely resembles the Irish Skean, as delineated in No. XIII. of *Collect. de Reb. Hib.* See fig. 3. 4. Plate II. It should

seem

preparing to take their oaths of fidelity before the lord marshal." *(r)* Indeed it should seem that the Beard was, at that time, cherished amongst the Irish, from the circumstance of the Beards of these Princes exciting the ridicule, and being wantonly plucked by some of John's attendants. *(s)* From this circumstance another conclusion may be deduced, that long Beards were not then worn in England, else those of the Irish would not have been matter of ridicule or surprize to the invaders *(t)*.

Soon after this weak prince had ascended the throne of his father, he made an attempt to introduce the English Dress amongst the Irish. According

---

seem from the following lines in *Hesperi-neso-graphia*, that the Irish sometimes wore the skean for a bloody purpose. The author describing his hero, Gillo, says,

> And at these fairs he ne'er was seen,
> Without a cudgel and a *Skean*;
> A cudgel of hard thorn or oak,
> With which he many craniums broke:
> With *Skean* he'd stab and charge about,
> And often let the blood come out.
>
> Canto 4.

(r) DAVIES's *Discov.* p. 37. Perhaps it may not be deemed impertinent to remark here, that when Jonathan was about to make a covenant with David, he put off his sword and his girdle. 1 *Sam.* ch. 18. HOWELL tells us, that by the old French proverb, " Il a quitté sa ceinture" was intimated, that a man had voluntarily forfeited his estate. *Fam. Lett.* p. 476.

(s) LELAND's *Hist. of Irel.* Vol. I. p. 144.

(t) This conclusion receives support from Mr. GRANGER. " After the conqueror " took possession of the kingdom, (says he) beards became unfashionable, and were pro- " bably looked upon as badges of disloyalty, as the Normans wore only whiskers." *Biog. Hist. of Engl.* Vol. I. p. 87. See also *An Hist. Essay on Beards*, p. 41.

THE DRESS OF THE IRISH.

cording to Rymer, he addressed an order to the archbishop of Dublin, directing him to buy such a quantity of Scarlets, as he should judge sufficient, to make robes to be presented to the Kings of Ireland, and others of the King's liege men, natives of the kingdom. These robes, Leland conjectures, were made after the English mode. " If so, (adds he) it " was by no means a contemptible device, to endeavour to habituate " their chiefs to the English garb; and, by their example, to render it " fashionable in their territories." *(u)* But John's policy failed on this, as well as on many other occasions.

In regard to my subject, the two succeeding reigns are shrouded with darkness; but amidst this darkness I have, however, been able to discern a sapphire sparkling on the finger of an archbishop of Dublin. In LIBER QUOTIDIANUS CONTRARATULATORIS GARDEROBÆ of 28 Edward I. there is enumerated *(v)* with other articles of Dress, a gold ring with a sapphire (anulus auri cum sapphiro) which had belonged to the archbishop of Dublin just then deceased.

In

(u) Hist. of Ireland. Vol. I. p. 195. Though the English might affect to despise the fashion of the Irish Dress at this time, yet we find them condescending to wear Irish manufactures. Amongst the different articles of Dress stolen at Winchester by Walter Bloweberme and Hamon le Stare, and which afterwards occasioned the celebrated duel between those gentlemen, about the close of this reign, was a tunic of Irish cloth. MADOX, *Hist. of the Exch.* p. 382. In fact, this country, so remarkably favourable to the linen manufacture, has not been less so to the woollen. This is acknowledged by that crafty and unfortunate statesman Thomas Earl of Strafford, who recommends to his sovereign the checking of the Woollen Manufacture on very illiberal grounds. Vide STRAFFORD's *Lett. and Disp.* Vol. II. p. 19. See also GOUGH's Edit. of CAMDEN's *Britan.* Vol. III. and DECKER's *Essay on Foreign Trade,* p. 156.

(v) Page 343. Col. VALLANCEY gives an high antiquity to the use of rings in Ireland, Vide *Vind. of the Anc. Hist. of Ireland,* p. 349. See also *Collect. de Reb. Hib.* No. XIII.

Plate

In the reign of Edward II. scarlet Cloaks and Collars (or Gorgets) continued to be worn by the Irish chieftains. Amongst the spoils left by the sons of Brien Roe, when they fled from Mortogh A. D. 1313, were shining scarlet Cloaks; and the Irish chiefs who joined Donagh against the English A. D. 1317, are described, closing their Collars when preparing for battle (*w*).

However rude the Irish Dress might have been in the reign of Edward III. it seems to have caught the fancy of the English settlers; for we find the use of it prohibited them in the celebrated statute of Kilkenny, passed during the administration of Edward's son, the duke of Clarence. One clause in this act ordains, " that the English here shall conform in " garb, and in the cut of their hair, to the fashion of their countrymen " in England; whoever affected that of the Irish, was to be treated as " such." On this clause my learned friend, the historian of Kilkenny, makes the following sensible observation: " Here is clearly dis-" closed the beginning degeneracy of the British colonies. Unrestrain-" ed by the wholesome severity of wise laws, and plunged in a perpetual " round of violence and rapine, they soon lost that manliness of senti-" ment and propriety of conduct they brought with them into the island; " they insensibly contracted a familiarity with, and a fondness for the " dissipated manners of the natives; they adopted their Dress, and look-" ed on the long Glibbs of this uncivilized people as their boast and " ornament" *(x)*. But my friend should not have stopped here; he should have further observed, that the vices and dissipated manners of

which

Plate XIV. and explanation. The Colonel has, in his possession, a silver ring for the finger, found in a bog near Athlone, with Egyptian characters on it.

(*w*) Vide *Annals of Inisf.* (M. S.)

(*x*) *Collect. de Reb. Hib.* Vol. II. p. 367.

THE DRESS OF THE IRISH.

which he complains, were occasioned by the oppressions of those very people who adopted them; by that " perpetual round of violence and rapine" in which they were plunged. This would have accounted for the uncouthness of the Irish Dress in the period before us, though it might not have justified the adoption of it by the English.

Yet finding, as I do, the inordinate use of Fur in Ireland restrained by an act passed at Westminster, in the 11th year of this reign, I am not sure that the epithet *uncouth*, which has just fallen from my pen, will apply in general to the apparel of the Irish at this period. I shall here transcribe the act to which I allude, as I find it in Ruffhead's edition of THE STATUTES AT LARGE, Vol. 1. p. 221. " Et auxint est
" acorde qe nul homme ne femme des dites terres d' Engleterre,
" Irlaund, Gales & Escoce deinz le poair nostre Seignur le Roi de
" quel estatou condition qil soit Rois Roynes & lor enfantz, prelatz,
" countes, barons, chivalers, dames & gentz de seinte eglise qi poent
" despendre par an cent livres au meins a la verroie value de lor benefices
" tantsoulement forpris ne use *Peleure en ses draps* qu serra achate apres
" la dite feste de feint Michel fur la forfaiture du pite peleure & outre
" destre puny a la volunte notre feignur le Roi."

Nor should it be forgotten, that another act was passed at Westminster, in the twenty-eighth year of this reign, for the encouragement of the manufacture and importation of Irish Frize, by exempting it from alnage, —" Item, ordeigne est et establi qe nulle subside ou aulnage soient
" paiez levez ne demandez des draps appellez *Frise-ware*, queux
" fount faitz en Ireland, &c." Hence we may infer, that even amidst the turbulence of the times, industry carried on her operations.

And hence we may alfo infer, that the ufeful arts were not now in the cradle, but had at leaft acquired the vigour of youth, elfe they could not have ftruggled fo fuccefsfully with the ftrong arm of the oppreffor.

But it is more, my lord, to our prefent purpofe to obferve, that a monument of the regal Drefs of this reign remains on St. Boyne's crofs *(z)* at Monafter-Boice, near Drogheda, Plate V. fig. 1. and that we are taught by this monument to believe, that the Irifh Kings at this time, wore the long Cota (or Shirt) and the Canabhas, faftened on the breaft with the Dealg-fallainne (or Broche ;) but, that the Truife, Hofe and Shoes, were articles of Drefs, which, like the ancient Romans, they affected to defpife.

Of the value of fome articles of drefs in this reign, the late publication of a brother academician enables me to fpeak with certainty. In the year 1339, he informs us, the prior of the commandery in Kilmainham-beg, in the county of Meath, allowed William de Marefchal, one of

the

(z) The date on the crofs is, A. D. 1328. Mr. BEAUFORD obferves, that the garment which I have called Cota in the text, was fometimes denominated a Sguird (or Shroud,) from inclofing the body, and was the general drefs of the chiefs and nobleffe, and therefore called by the old Irifh, Conach, Eneach or Dunlatha, that is, the drefs of the chief. In the *Statutes of Man*, it is denominated, Camifia. It was ufually girt round the body by a girdle, and then had fome refemblance to the Highland Filleadthbeg, and the original of the old Englifh Paltoc, yet retained in fome meafure by the battle-axe guards. Befides the figure at Monafter-Boice, there is another regal figure on a tomb in the abbey of Strade (co. Mayo) of which the body appears to be only covered with a fhort cloak, faftened over the breaft with a Broche. Of this figure a drawing is now in my poffeffion.

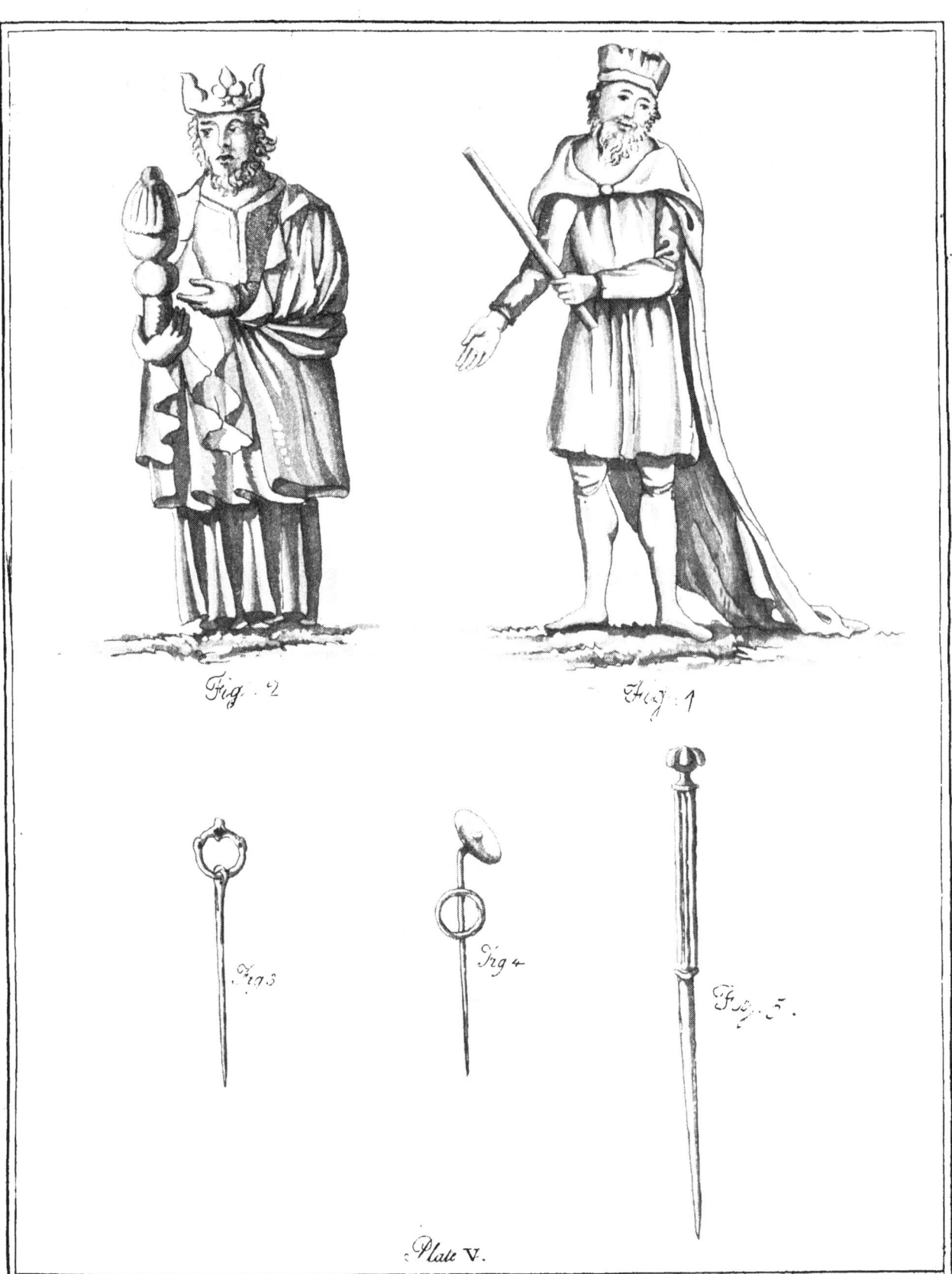

Plate V.

THE DRESS OF THE IRISH.

the knights retained by the commandery, 40s. for his own robe full trimmed; 20s. for clothing his esquire for two years; and 10s. for clothing each of his chamberlains, during the same period; and, to William Reddelyn, one of his own retainers, he allowed, annually, 10s. in silver, for cloths, and 5s. for shoes *(a)*. And, during this reign, according to the same authority, the prior of Kilmainham granted, every second year, to master Walter Islip, whom he agreed to entertain in the priory, 20s. in silver for clothing his chaplain; 40s. for his two armigers; and two marks for his two other servants *(b)*.

The dress, or rather the appearance of an Irish Prince in the following reign, is thus described by a gentleman who accompanied Richard II. to Ireland. " Among othir gentilmen (says my author) I was one
" that went with him (the earl of Gloucester) to see M^c. Morough, his
" behaviour, estate, and forces, and to what issue the treaty would
" grow unto. Between two woodes, not far from the sea, M^c. Mo-
" rough, (attendid by multitudes of the Irish) descended from a moun-
" tain, mounted upon a horse without a saddle, which cost him (as it
" was reported) four hundrith cows.—His horse was fair, and in his
" descent from the hill to us, he ran as swift as any stagg, hare, or the
" swiftest beast that I have seen. In his right hand he bear a great
" long dart, which he cast from him with much dexterity.—He was
" tall of stature, well composed, strong and active. His countenance

fierce

(a) Monast. Hib. p. 552. 553.

(b) Ibid. p. 233.

"fierce and cruel" *(c)*. But that moſt entertaining of all chroniclers, Froiſſart, whom we find in the ſuite of Richard, in one of his Iriſh expeditions, thus more minutely deſcribes the Dreſs of the four Iriſh Kings who ſwore allegiance to his royal maſter. " Encores auoyent ils
" un uſage, qui bien ſauoye qu'ils ont communement en leur pais. C'eſt
" qu'ils ne portens nulles *brayes* : je leur fei faire des draps linges grand
" foiſon ; et en fei delivrer aux Roys & a leur gors : & les remei en
" celui uſaye : et leur oſtay durant le terme qui je fu avecques aux,
" moult de choſes rudes & mal appartenans, tans d'habits, comme
" d'autres choſes : & a trop grand different leur vint, du premier, de
" veſter houpelandes de draps de ſoye, faurries de menu vers & de gris
" *(d)*, car, au devant, ces Roys eſtoyent bien paris d' affluber *un mantel*
" *d' Irelande* *(e)*. Ils cheauchoyent ſans *ſelle ſommiers*, and ſans nuls
" *extriers* *(f)*."

That

(c) HARRIS' *Hib.* p. 53. The Dreſs of Mac Murrough and his attendants on this occaſion, is thus deſcribed by STRUTT from an ancient painting. " Mac. Murrough has a light pink robe over his ſhoulders ; and the figure next to him is in white, with a red cap; and the third figure is in red, with a white cap. The middlemoſt figure of the foldiers is in red, and the other two in blue." *Reg. and Eccl. Antiq. of Engl.* p. 17.

(d) Gris.—Lord BERNIER tranſlates this word, Grai. But that is too vague a tranſlation. Let us hear the learned editor of BLOUNT's *Ancient Tenures.* " Gris was an animal, but not known, as I take it, in England. The fur, however, was in eſteem here." p. 131. See alſo MADOX' *Hiſt. of the Exch.* p. 253. and TYRWHITT's *Chaucer*, Vol. IV. p. 200.

(e) The deſcription is illuſtrated by fig. 1. in Plate V.

(f) Tom. IV. p. 203. ed. par SAVAARY.

THE DRESS OF THE IRISH.

That the want of Saddles, Stirrups and Bridles, amongst the Irish, should be so particularly noticed by our travellers, is not to be wondered at, as they were then, and had been, for many years before, in general use in England, (*g*) and on the Continent. But, it appears from some BREHON LAWS in the Seabright COLLECTION, that these necessary articles of horse furniture had only fallen into disuetude in Ireland. As these laws have not yet been published, I shall make no apology for arresting the course of this little history, in order to introduce them here.

" Sriden oir, no airgid gacha airigh ro shuigheadh i comhoire, im comhul geallaibh; penaicer acht i rechail.—*A golden or silver bridle* to every Airech is to be paid in horses."

" Ailib srian gacha og airich, agus gacha bo airicheach cumhal; eghta mna fuillem la aichghin i rein.—The *bridle* of every Ogairech and of every Boairech, is a cumal of horses; the value of the bridles of their wives, the same."

" Srian cacha, airech-feibe, diliongbe, hech cumal beich sec; mna, fuillem la oichgin i rein.—The *bridle* of every Airech-feibhe is a cumal of horses, worth six or ten cows; that of his wife, the same."

" Fuillem gill longe caire Cacha airech-febe ro suibiged for beich secaibh, la aichgin, mad long caire rig ro ruibibe for richehihicc fec la aichgin.—The value of a long-caire (or *stirrup*) to every Airech-feibhe, is ten cows; and to a King, twenty cows."

But

(*g*) See MADOX' *Hist. and Antiq. of the Excheq.* p. 250. 252.

But to return:—Uncouth as the Dress of the Irish in the period from which we just digressed, might have seemed to a polished Frenchman, it appears from the following passage of a neglected Italian author of this age (whom your Lordship has had the merit of bringing to light), that they now supplied materials for the dress of other nations.

> Similimente passamo en Irlanda,
> La qual fra noi e degna de Fama
> Per le nobile SAIE *(h)* che ci manda *(i)*.

Nor did that passage in Rymer's FŒDERA elude your Lordship's learned researches, in which he informs us, that, in a licence granted to the Pope's agent, A. D. 1482, Ann. 5. Rich. II. for exporting into Italy certain commodities custom-free, we may find the following articles of Irish

(h) In the learned Essay which incited me to this attempt, it is observed, that in Article SAIA in *Dict. della Crusca*, there is quoted an ancient account-book called *Quattre Contre*, in which is the following article; " Per un pezza di *Saia* d' Irlanda per vestir della moglie d'Andrea."——In an act passed in England, in 12 Will. III. we find the exportation of Sayes from Ireland prohibited; but in the reign of Queen Anne, they were again admitted to duty, according to a *Book of Rates* of that reign.

(i) *Dittamondi*, componuto per FAZIO DELLI UBERTI. Capitula 26. printed 1474. —" In like manner we pass into Ireland, which among us is worthy of renown for the excellent *serges* that she sends us."

Plate VII.

Irish woollens, viz. five mantles of *Irish cloth*, one lined with green; one ruffet garment lined with *Irish cloth* (*j*).

The female Dress of this period, has been happily preserved on a tomb in the priory of Athassel. After removing an heap of rubbish, a friend of mine, who had made Irish sculpture his study, discovered on this tomb a female figure rudely sculptured, which he gives to the age before us. The hair is reticulated round the forehead, in a manner as formal and unbecoming, as the head-dress of the old maid in Hogarth's MORNING. On her breast appears a solitaire, from which an ornament is pendent. Her right hand holds a glove; and with her left, she supports her train. Plate VI. fig. 1. (*k*) In the monastery of St. Saviour at Ross, in the county of Wexford, there is a monumental figure in a similar dress of Rose Macrue, at whose expence the town was walled in, A. D. 1310. This figure also holds a glove (*l*) in one hand.

But

(*j*) Vol. VII. p. 136.

(*k*) There was no date on the tomb, at least my friend could discover none. But the figure being in a dress resembling that of Rose Macrue does, in some degree, determine the age of the monument in question, and support the conjecture of my friend. Besides, trains were worn at this period by the English ladies. Vide GOUGH's *Sepulch. Mon. of Great Brit.* Introd. p. 128.

(*l*) The glove was probably intended to denote the exalted rank of the deceased, as it was formerly customary in England to inter the Kings and nobility with gloves on their hands. Vide Ibid. and HEARNE's *Curious Disc.* v. 1. p. 203. 211. If we may infer that gloves were actually worn by Rose Macrue, and the lady buried at Athassel, they must have been in use amongst the Irish ladies, before they became an article of female Dress

in

But the use of the Glove was not now entirely confined to the fair: it should seem from the following passage in the history of THE ANTIQUITIES OF IRISHTOWN AND KILKENNY, that it sometimes covered the holy hand of ecclesiastics. "Bishop Snell (who died in the year 1416) "bestowed on the cathedral some rich presents, as *Gloves*, pontifical "sandals, a silken caphin, interwoven with gold spots, and a mitre "adorned with precious stones" *(m)*. From this passage, it should also seem, that even in those ages of simplicity, the ministers of the Gospel were no enemies to the glare of Dress.

The fashion of the Beard, as worn in Ireland during the reign of Henry VI. may be learned from the following act of parliament, intituled, AN ACT THAT HE THAT WILL BE TAKEN FOR AN ENGLISHMAN, SHALL NOT USE A BEARD UPON HIS UPPER LIP ALONE, THE OFFENDER SHALL BE TAKEN AS AN IRISH ENEMY *(n)*. "For that, that now there is no diversity in array "betwixt the English marchours, and the Irish enemies, and so by "colour of the English marchours, the Irish enemies do come from day "to day, to other into the English counties as English marchours, and

do

in England; for Mr. GOUGH informs us, that gloves seem to have been no part of female Dress in England till after the Reformation. Introd. p. 184.

(m) Collect de Reb. Hib. Vol. II. p. 458. Of the finery of the Cloister we have earlier mention in *The Annals of Innisfallen*, (MS.) Under the year 1305, we are told, that when the abbey of Ennis was fully perfected by Turlogh the founder, he provided it with a sanctuary, furnished with cowls for Friars, and veils for Nuns, costly and beautifully wrought.

(n) Rot. Parl. cap. 20. I have been confidently assured, that the grand-father of the right honourable John O'Neil, the present elegant and accomplished proprietor of Shane's-Castle, always wore his Beard after the prohibited Irish mode.

" do rob and pill by the high ways, and deſtroy the common people
" by lodging upon them in the nights, and alſo do kill the huſbands
" in the nights, and do take their goods to the Iriſhmen: wherefore
" it is ordained and agreed, that no manner man that will be taken for
" an Engliſhman, ſhall have no beard above his mouth, that is to ſay,
" that he have no hairs upon his upper lip, ſo that the ſaid lip be once
" at leaſt ſhaven every forthnight, or of equal growth with the neather
" lip. And if any man be found amongſt the Engliſh contrary hereunto,
" that then, it ſhall be lawful to every man to take them, and their
" goods as Iriſh enemies, and to ranſom them as Iriſh enemies."

And from another act of parliament paſſed in the ſame reign, we learn, that, though Bridles and Saddles were rather ſcarce in Ireland in the time of Richard II. that it now became neceſſary to prohibit the uſe of gilt Bridles and Peytrels. I ſhall here tranſcribe the act (*o*).
" For that, that the clipping of the King our ſovereign lord's coyn hath
" cauſed divers men in this land of Ireland to counterfeit the ſame
coin,

(*o*) Intituled, *An act againſt clipped money, money called O'Reyley's money, and other unlawful money, and againſt gilt Bridles, and Peytrels, and other gilt Harneſs.* Rot. Parl. cap. 22. Not many years ſince, the bit and headſtal of a bridle, both of braſs, were found in the county of Roſcommon, and are now in the muſeum of the Univerſity of Dublin. They are thus deſcribed by colonel VALLANCEY in *Collect. de Reb. Hib.* No. XIII. p. 54. who has illuſtrated his deſcription with an engraving. " The bitt is of extraordinary neat and curious work-
" manſhip: a celebrated artiſt of Dublin, aſſured me, that it was impoſſible to make a
" better joint, at this day, than that of the centre of the bitt. The curb and chains
" were of gold, but were ſecreted by the peaſant who found it. On the top of the head-
" ſtall, an elegant pillar of braſs is erected, to which a plume of feathers was faſten-
" ed." And, in a bog near Burnham-Caſtle in the county of Kerry, was found a large braſs ſpur, formerly gilt. CAMDEN's *Brit.* apud GOUGH, Vol. III.

"coin, to the great hurt and destruction of the said land, and the
"making of gilt bridles and peytrels (*o*) hath also wasted and con-
"sumed the gold of the said land for the more part, and is like to do
"more hereafter, if it be not speedily remedied: Wherefore it is ordain-
"ed and agreed by authority of this present parliament, that no money
"so clipped be received in any place of the said land, from the first day
"of May next to come (1447), nor the money called O'Reyley's mo-
"ney, or any other unlawful money, so that one coyner be ready at the
"said day to make the coyne. And also that no man be so hardy hence-
"forward to use any gilt bridles, peytrells, nor any other gilt harneys in
"no place of the said land; excepted knights and prelates of holy
"churches. And if any man be found with any such bridle, peytrell,
"or other harneys gilted from the same day, that it be lawful to every
"man that will, to take the said man, his horse and harneys and to
"possess the same as his own goods."

Mr. Steevens, in some of his learned researches, discovered an act of parliament passed at Trim in this reign (A. D. 1446), in which the natives were among other things restricted from wearing shirts stained with saffron (*p*). The motive of this prohibition I can neither conceive, nor learn; nor can I find the act alluded to (*q*). The Irish, however,

as

(*o*) Peytrell.—Fr. The breast-plate of an horse. TYRWHITT's *Cant. Tales.* Gloss.

(*p*) STEEVEN's *Shakespeare*, Vol. IV. p. 128.

(*q*) It does not appear in Dr. VESEY's edition of the *Irish Statutes at large*. But several acts of parliament passed in this kingdom during, and prior to this reign, are either totally lost, or buried in the dust of libraries. Vide MOLYNEUX' *Case of Irel.* p. 27. Dub. Ed. 1782.

THE DRESS OF THE IRISH.

as we shall see, continued to stain their shirts with saffron so low as the reign of Elizabeth (*r*); for no custom, as an elegant writer observes, how absurd soever it may be, if it has subsisted long, or derives its force from the manners and prejudices of the age in which it prevails, was ever abolished by the bare promulgation of laws and statutes.

The female dress of this reign is neither enshrined in a statute, nor embalmed by history; but it lives in marble. In the ruins of St. Mary's church, picturesquely situated over the sea on the north side of the peninsula of Howth, stands the tomb of Christopher, 13th baron of Howth (*s*), on which is cumbent the effigy of his wife Anne Plunket, whose dress is faithfully delineated in Plate VII. fig. 1. As the church is unroofed, the weather has acted freely on the tomb; so that it was impossible when I viewed it, and had it sketched a few weeks since, to follow every stroke of the chisel. But I could clearly discover the reticulated head-dress, and trace imperfectly some elegant ornaments on the girdle. In the cross, which has escaped the injuries of time, is probably preserved the form of one, once adorned with gems, which, while it sparkled on the breast,

" —— Jews might kiss, and Infidels adore."

Indulging

(*r*) CAMPION tells us, that when he wrote his *History of Ireland* (1571) saffron was beginning to fall into disuse, p. 18.—Castle-Saffron, in the county of Cork, was so called from the quantity of saffron formerly cultivated there by the Irish, for dying their habits. SMITH's *Hist. of the Co. of Cork*.

(*s*) From an inscription on the tomb we learn, that he died A. D. 1430.

Indulging this notion, I stood for some time, wrapt in pleasing meditation over the tomb.

In the reign of Edward IV. it was the interest of an Irishman who was inclined to rob or murder his neighbour, to wear the English apparel, as he might commit those atrocious crimes with impunity, under the sanction of that garb, agreeably to AN ACT THAT IT SHALL BE LAWFUL TO KILL ANY THAT IS FOUND ROBBING BY DAY OR NIGHT, OR GOING OR COMING TO ROB OR STEAL, HAVING NO FAITHFUL MAN OF GOOD NAME OR FAME IN THEIR COMPANY IN ENGLISH APPAREL (t).

But this indulgence not proving a sufficiently strong inducement to the Irish, to dress after the English mode, it was thought necessary, by the same gracious Prince, to pass AN ACT THAT THE IRISHMEN DWELLING IN THE COUNTIES OF DUBLIN, MYETH, URIEL, AND KILDARE, SHALL GO APPARELLED LIKE ENGLISHMEN, AND WEAR THEIR BEARDS AFTER THE ENGLISH MANNER, SWEAR ALLEGIANCE, AND TAKE ENGLISH SURNAMES (u).

The ladies, however, were permitted to indulge their fancy, and we find them dressing with elegance and taste. On the tomb of sir Rowland Eustace at New-Abbey in the county of Kildare, which bears date 1476 (w), are two female figures. Plate VIII. fig. 1. 2. which my friend

Mr.

(t) Rot. Parl. cap. 12.

(u) Ibid. cap. 16.

(w) This abbey was founded A. D. 1460, by Sir Richard Eustace, whose lady, Margaret Janico, is represented in fig. 1.

THE DRESS OF THE IRISH.

Mr. Beauford, in a letter to me, thus describes: "The lady with a girdle
"(fig. 1.), has on her head a cap denominated by the Irish, Curach, by
"the French, Coronette, and by the English, Cornet; it was worn by
"ladies of fashion, throughout the western parts of Europe, from the
"12th to the 15th century. The veil which hangs down behind the
"figure, and seems intended to have been drawn, occasionally, over the
"face, varied in length according to the prevailing mode (x). Petrarch des-
"cribes his Laura as frequently dressed in one of them. The fillet or bor-
"der which went over the forehead, and which was usually ornamented
"with gold and silver needle work, and with precious stones, was deno-
"minated by the Irish, Cabhien or Ciebhien, by the English, Frontlet,
"and by the old French, Frontliere. The gown of this figure was
"worn by most of the western nations during the 14th and 15th centu-
"ries, and was called by the Irish a Cartall or Kertle, and is mentioned
"in some of our statutes."

"The weeping figure," he continues, (fig. 2.) "has on her forehead
"the Cabhien, over which is drawn the veil, denominated by the English,
"Kercher

(x) A lady, to whom I am indebted for many useful hints, seems to think that the veil was in general use amongst the early Irish. Her grounds for this presumption, she has condescended to mention, in one of the valuable letters with which she was pleased to honor me, during the progress of this work. "Looking on romances and works of fancy to be "the best materials to form a judgment by, concerning the manners and fashions of the "age in which they were written, (says she) I have had several translated from the Irish. "From these it appears, that veils were worn by the younger persons amongst the ancient "Irish. And, that the garments consisted of many folds or plaits, with richer personages, "(she continues) may be inferred from the frequent expression in those romances of the "*seven fold robe of Scarlet.*"

"Kercher (*y*), and by the Irish, Seol (pronounced shawl) (*z*), and by the old French, Carchoire or Kerchoire. It was not peculiar to the Irish, being worn equally by the French and English women during the 13th and 14th centuries. Under the Seol, the figure wears the mantle called by the Irish Cocculach, Falachclioback and Gaunaca. Beneath this, on the shoulders, she has the Cliobhach (or cloak) worn at present by the Highland women. Her under garment consists of the Kertal or Kertle" (*a*).

In the reign of Henry VII. sir Edward Poynings, in order, says sir John Davies, that the parliaments of Ireland might want no decent or honourable form that was used in England, caused a particular act to pass, that the lords of Ireland should appear in the like parliament Robes as the English lords are wont to wear in the parliaments of England (*b*).

This

(*y*) In England the kercher or kerchief was made of linen, and worn by both sexes. See p. 350. of that scarce and valuable work, *The Household book of the Earl of Northumberland*. The kerchief was an head cover. Vide PINKERTON's *Anc. Scot. Poems*. Gloss.

(*z*) Vide *Vind. of the Anc. Hist. of Irel.* p. 118. for some learned observations on this word.

(*a*) Kertel.—Sax. a tunic or waistcoat. TYRWHITT, *Cant. Tales*. Gloss. A Close gown.—PINKERTON, *Anc. Scot. Poems*. Gloss. In the poem of *Chrystis Kirk of the Grene*, the kirtle is thus described,

> Thair kirtillis wer of Lynkome licht,
> Weil prest with mony plaitis.

(*b*) *Davies' Disc.* p. 186. oct. ed.

THE DRESS OF THE IRISH.

This act is entitled, A STATUTE FOR THE LORDS OF THE PARLIAMENT TO WEAR ROBES (*c*). And the penalty for offending againſt it, was a C. s. to be levied off the offenders lands and goods.

While the reign of Henry VII. is under conſideration, I ſhall tranſcribe a paſſage for my purpoſe from THE HISTORY AND ANTIQUITIES OF IRISHTOWN AND KILKENNY. " There is, (ſays my author) a
" warm diſpute in THE RED BOOK of Kilkenny, in the 6th Hen. VII.
" between the glovers and ſhoemakers, about the right of making gir-
" dles and all manner of girdles ; which is at once a collateral proof of
" the looſe garments worn in this age, (*d*) and how profitable in conſe-
" quence was the employment here contended for. The rich (he conti-
" nues) had alſo their whole cloth, extremely fine, that had paſſed the
" alnage; for ſo, pannum integrum de Aſſiſa, may be interpreted ; alſo
" their cloth of gold, their bodkins or tiſſues, their ſilks and taffates" (*e*).
In order to account for the finding ſuch mercery in an Iriſh town in this century, our author tells us, " we are not to forget, that the frequent
" concourſe of the nobility to this place (Kilkenny) beſides the taſte of
" the times (*f*), was the obvious cauſe for introducing theſe commodi-
" ties.

(*c*) Rot. Parl. cap. 30.

(*d*) The old Earl of Kildare, who was attainted in the parliament of 1359, uſually rode in a large looſe ſcarlet cloak. HOLINGSHED's *Chron. of Irel.* p. 100.

(*e*) *Collect. de Reb. Hib.* Vol. II. p. 383.

(*f*) The taſte of the times certainly led to great expence. For, when the caſtle of Maynooth was taken by William Brereton in 1534, honeſt HOLINGHED tells us, that, " great and rich was the ſpoile, ſuch ſtore of beds, ſo manie goodlie hangings, ſo rich
" a ward-

48 AN HISTORICAL ESSAY ON

" ties. The poorer fort had their Irifh ftuffs, called falewyche and
" wyrfted, their canvas linen, their Phallangs, and Mantles; felt caps
" are alfo mentioned" (*g*).

Nor fhould I omit to notice a bequeft made in this reign, which fir James Ware has recorded in his ANNALS, " 1499. Died, John Savage,
" who had been mayor of Dublin in the year 1493: he bequeathed to
" Chrift-church, Dublin, *two veftments of purple velvet*, with a *Cope* (*h*)
" of the fame."—An offering, made in this church, a few years after, has an equal claim to our notice.—" 1506. On the firft of November,
" Gerald earl of Kildare, made an offering in this church of *two veft-*
" *ments of cloth of gold, and tuffy*" (*i*).

Although my refearches have been fedulous, I have not been able to difcover the fafhion of the Coïffure worn on this fide the grave by the Irifh ladies, during the reign before us; but, the head-drefs in which they defcended into the tomb, appears on a monumental figure of the family of the Butlers, at Fertagh, in the county of Kilkenny, Plate IX. fig. 1. (*k*). The reft of the figure is wrapped in a fhroud. Nothing has occurred to me more fimilar to this coif, than the mitred head-drefs worn in England

" a wardrobe, fuch brave furniture, as trulie it was accounted (for houfhold ftuffe and
" utenfiles) one of the richeft earle his houfes under the crowne of England." *Chron. of Irel.* p. 95.

(*g*) *Collect. de Reb. Hib.* Vol. II. p. 384.

(*h*) Cope.—A cloak worn on facred miniftrations by a clergyman. WHITAKER.

(*i*) *Obituary* of Chrift Church, Dublin, (MS.)

(*k*) The date on the tomb is 1489.

Plate 9.

land about the twelfth and thirteenth centuries (*l*), and even that bears but an imperfect resemblance to it. The singularity of this head-dress struck bishop Pococke; but he offers no conjecture on it, and only describes it as rising up on each side, in two horns *(m)*.

Henry VIII. having dispatched some of his wives, and several of his favourites, and seized himself of the most valuable possessions of the church, began to turn his thoughts towards Ireland. " Perpending and
" waying by his great wisdom, learning and experience, how much it
" doth more conferre to the induction of rude and ignorant people to
" the knowledge of Almighty God, and of the good and vertuous obe-
" dience, which by his most holy precepts and commandements they
" owe to their princes and superiours, then a good instruction in his most
" blessed laws, with a conformitie, concordance and familiarity in lan-
" guage, tongue, in manners, order, and apparel, with them that be
" civil people" (*n*), directed an act to be passed (*o*), ordaining, " That
" no person, ne persons, the King's subjects within this land (Ireland)
" being, or hereafter to be, from and after the first day of May, which
" shall

(*l*) Gough's *Sepulch. Monum. of Great Brit.* Vol. I. p. 30.

(*m*) *Monast. Hib.* p. 350.

(*n*) Preamble of the act.

(*o*) Intituled, *An act for the English order, habite and language.* Rot. Parl. cap. 26. Henry, who, as Mr. Walpole observes, dictated in every thing, from religion to fashion, had likewise a sumptuary act of parliament passed in the 24th year of his reign, respecting the dress of his English subjects. *Anec: of Paint. in Engl.* Vol. I. p. 222. oct. ed.

"shall be in the yeare of our Lord God 1539, shall be shorn, or shaven
"above the ears, or use the wearing of haire upon their heads, like unto
"long lockes, called glibbes, or have or use any haire growing on their
"upper lippes, called or named a crommeal, or use or weare any shirt,
"smock, kerchor, bendel, neckerchour, mocket or linnen cappe, coloured,
"or dyed with saffron, ne yet use, or wear in any their shirts or
"smockes above seven yards of cloth, to be measured according to the
"King's standard, and that also no woman use or wear any kyrtell or
"cote tucked up (*p*), or imbroydred or garnished with silke (*q*), or
"couched ne layd with usker, after the Irish fashion; and that no person
"or persons of what estate, condition, or degree they be, shall use or
"weare any mantles, cote or hood made after the Irish fashion, and if any
"person or persons use or weare any shirt, smock, cote, hood, mantle,
kircher,

(*p*) What particular fashion is alluded to by the expression of "cote tucked up," I know not; for it appears, as well from the evidences of ancient romances, as from tradition, that the Irish ladies of the higher ranks formerly wore flowing trains, which were sometimes borne up by a page. In the romance of the *Death of Cucholin*, (already quoted,) the queen Mieve is represented as putting on "a five-fold Scarlet robe."—And an old lady, now living in the county of Westmeath, remembers to have once fallen, during her infancy, into the company of madam O'Reilly, commonly called the countess of Cavan, the last of that unfortunate house. The only part of the dress of this venerable dame that made an impression on the infant mind of my informant, was her train, of which the length was so considerable, as to spread incommodiously across the floor of the drawing-room. One of the company happening to step incautiously on the end of it, the old lady turned round and said, with an heavy sigh, "alas! I once had a page to bear up my train."

(*q*) In the Erse poem of *Oran eadar Ailte agus Mac-Ronain air dhoibh fearg a ghabhail ri Fionn*, lately published, by my learned friend Dr. YOUNG, the female ambassador from the Irish King is described as having two golden apples in her right hand, and ornaments on the shoulder of her gown, and the *form of a tree inwoven*. *Trans. of the Roy. Irish Acad.* for 1787. Antiq. p. 88.

THE DRESS OF THE IRISH.

" kercher, bendell, neckerchor, mocket, or linnen cap, contrary to
" the forme above recited, that then every perfon fo offending, fhall
" forfeit the thing fo ufed or worne, and that it fhall be lawfull to every
" the King's true fubjects, to feize the fame; and further, the offendor
" in any of the premiffes, fhall forfeit for every time fo wearing the
" fame againft the forme aforefaid, fuch penalties and fummes of mo-
" ny as hereafter by this prefent act is limited and appointed (r)."

From this act we learn, that the art of Embroidery, fo much encouraged by the Irifh legiflature at the commencement of the Chriftian Æra,
was ftill cultivated by our anceftors *(s)*; and that the ufe of filk, fo often

---

(r) This Statute feems, from baron FINGLAS's *Breviate*, to have been beft obferved in the counties of Kerry, Waterford, Cork, Limerick, Kilkenny, and Tipperary. Vide HARRIS' *Hib.* p. 102, 103. oct. ed. And from this *Breviate* we alfo learn, that in this age the works of the loom were the employment of women. " Item, that noo merchaunts " wife ufe any tavern of ale upon pain of twenty fhillings, toties quoties, as oftin any " of theme do the contrary; but lett theme be occupied *in making of woollen cloath* " *and linnen.*" Ibid. p. 99. Indeed I am inclined to think, with a learned friend, that as well in the early, as in the middle ages, the fhuttle was ufually thrown in Ireland, by the hand of the Fair. In thofe fimple ages, almoft every female accomplifhment had utility for its object.

(s) Even the habits of the retainers of the Irifh nobility in this reign, were fometimes embroidered with filk. It is related by Holinfhed, that, while chancellor Cromer was en-
deavouring,

ten mentioned in the BREHON LAWS, and in the songs of our early Bards, still prevailed amongst them :---and by this act we are in some degree taught, not only the fashions of this period, but of the middle ages in general.

After the reign of Henry VIII. I cannot find that the reform of the Irish Dress became an object of parliamentary consideration; nor were the statutes respecting it put into force; it was now left to the influence of fashion. Yet Spencer, with his usual eloquence, in his VIEW OF THE STATE OF IRELAND, thus strongly recommends the abolition of the ancient Dress, which it seems continued to prevail in the reign of Elizabeth.

Irenæus having shewn the various uses of the Mantle, is asked by Eudoxus, "what reason have you then to wish so necessary a thing cast "off?" To this he replies, "because the commodity doth not countervail "the discommodity; for the inconveniencies which thereby do arise, are "much more many; for it is a fit house for an out-law, a meet bed for "a rebel, and an apt cloke for a thief. First, the out-law, being for his
"many

---

deavouring, by all the arts of eloquence, to dissuade lord Thomas (son of the then earl of Kildare) from rebellious purposes, " one Bard de Nelan, an Irish rithmour, was chatting " of Irish verses, as though his toong had run on pattens, in commendation of the lord " Thomas, investing him with the title of *Silken Thomas,* because his *horsemens Jacks* " *were gorgeouslie imbrodered with silk.*"—*Chron. of Irel.* p. 91.

THE DRESS OF THE IRISH.

" many crimes and villanies banished from the towns and houses of
" honest men, and wandring in waste places, far from danger of law,
" maketh his Mantle his house, and under it covereth himself from the
" wrath of heaven, from the offence of the earth, and from the sight of
" men. When it raineth, it is his pent-house; when it bloweth, it is
" his tent; when it freezeth, it is his tabernacle. In summer, he can
" wear it loose; in winter, he can wrap it close; at all times he can use
" it; never heavy, never cumbersome. Likewise for a rebel it is as ser-
" viceable: for in his war that he maketh (if at least it deserve the
" name of war) when he still flieth from his foe, and lurketh in the
" thick woods, and strait passages, waiting for advantages, it is his
" bed, yea, and almost his household-stuff. For the wood is his house
" against all weathers, and his Mantle is his couch to sleep in: Therein
" he wrappeth himself round, and coucheth himself strongly against the
" gnats, which, in that countrey, do more annoy the naked rebels, whilst
" they keep the woods, and do more sharply wound them, than all
" their enemies swords or spears, which can seldom come nigh them.
" Yea, and oftentimes their Mantle serveth them, when they are near dri-
" ven, being wrapped about their left arm, in stead of a target; for it is hard
" to cut through with a sword, besides, it is light to bear, light to throw
" away, and being (as they commonly are) naked, it is to them all in
" all. Lastly, for a thief, it is so handsome, as it may seem it was first
" invented for him; for under it he may cleanly convey any fit pillage
" that cometh handsomely in his way; and when he goeth abroad in
" the night free-booting, it is his best and surest friend; for lying, as they
" often do, two or three nights together abroad, to watch for their booty,
" with that they can prettily shroud themselves under a bush or a bank
" side, till they may conveniently do their errand: And when all is over, he

" can,

"can, in his Mantle, pass through any town or company, being close
"hooded over his head (*u*) as he useth, from knowledge of any to
"whom he is endangered. Besides this, he, or any man else, that is
"disposed to mischief or villany, may, under his Mantle, go privily arm-
"ed, without suspicion of any, carry his head-piece, his skean, or pistol,
"if he please, to be always in readiness. Thus necessary and fitting is
"a Mantle for a bad man, and surely for a bad house-wife, it is no less
"convenient; for some of them that be wandring women, called of
"them Mona-Shull, it is half a wardrobe; for in summer, you shall find
"her

(*u*) There is an evident allusion to the custom of occasionally covering the head with the mantle as a disguise, in a beautiful inedited Irish romance in the collection of the countess of MOIRA, entitled, Eachtra Faṗbhlaiḋh, ingheaṅ riġh Alban, 7 Cheaṗbhuill mhic Donchaiḋh mhóir ui Ḋhaluiġh, (*The adventures of Faravla, Princess of Scotland, and Carval O' Daly*), with a translation of which, the accomplished possessor has been pleased to favour me.—Faravlas' father having discovered that Carval, while on a visit at his palace, aspired to the hand of his daughter, whose affections he had gained, threw him into prison and condemned him to death. " At this (says my author) Faravla
" threw off all restraint: she wept, and mourned; neglected bathing, and refused nou-
" rishment. The next morning being appointed for his execution, she covered her face
" with her robe, and going to the prison, gained, by gifts and entreaties, permission from
" his guard to take a last farewell of her lover. Upon entering the apartment, she desired
" the guards to watch at the door, and give her notice if any person approached. Gained
" by her liberality, and knowing that she must reign after her father's decease, they com-
" plied. Faravla then caused Carval immediately to change garments with her, and *shewed
" him how to cover his face with his robe*, and lying down in the place of Carval, he was
" let out by the guard as Faravla."—In baron FINGLAS' *Breviate*, it is recommended,
" that noo Englishman of the londe weare *overslipp Irish coate and hood* on payne of an hun-
" dreth shillings, toties quoties." In his prohibited custom probably originated the epithet, *rug-headed*, which Shakespear somewhere applies to the Irish kerns; as the mantle of the vulgar Irish were generally made of rug. See MORYSON's *Itin*. Part. 3. p. 101.

"her arrayed commonly, but in her smock and mantle, to be more ready for her light services; in winter, and in her travail, it is her cloak and safeguard, and also a coverlet for her lewd exercise. And when she hath filled her vessel, under it she can hide both her burden, and her blame; yea, and when her bastard is born, it serves instead of swadling clouts. And as for all other good women which love to do but little work, how handsome it is to lye in and sleep, or to louse themselves in the sun-shine, they that have been but a while in Ireland can well witness. Sure I am, that you will think it very unfit for a good huswife to stir in, or busie herself about her huswifry in such sort as she should. These be some of the abuses for which I would think it meet to forbid all Mantles." Nor is he a greater friend to the Glibbs which he thinks " as fit masks as a Mantle is for a thief. "For whensoever (says he) he hath run himself into that peril of law, that he will not be known, he either cutteth off his glibb quite, by which he becometh nothing like himself, or pulleth it so low down over his eyes, that it is very hard to discern his thievish countenance."

But Spencer himself gives some good reasons, afterwards, for dispensing with the observance of those laws. The passage, which contains some further particulars of the Irish Dress, is, though long, too curious to be omitted.

"Eudox. But are there not laws already provided for avoiding of this evil?

"Iren. Yes, I think there be; but as good never a whit as never "the better: for what do Statutes avail without penalties, or laws with-
"out

"out charge of execution? For so there is another like law enacted
"against wearing of the Irish apparel, but neverthemore is it observed by
"any, or executed by them that have the charge: for they in their pri-
"vate discretions think it not fit to be forced upon the poor wretches of
"that countrey, which are not worth the price of English apparel, nor ex-
"pedient to be practised against the abler sort, by reason that the coun-
"try (say they) doth yield no better; and were there better to be had,
"yet these were fitter to be used; as namely, the Mantle in travelling,
"because there be no inns where meet bedding may be had, so that his
"mantle serves him then for a bed. The leather quilted jack in jour-
"neying and in camping, for that it is fittest to be under his shirt of
"male, and for any occasion of sudden service, as there happen many,
"to cover his trouse on horseback. The great linen roll, which the wo-
"men wear, to keep their heads warm, after cutting their hair, which
"they use in any sickness. Besides their thick-folded linen shirts, their
"long-sleeved smocks, their half-sleeved coats, their silken fillets, and
"all the rest, they will devise some colour for, either of necessity, or of
"antiquity, or of comeliness" *(y)*.

But in order to give your lordship a still more precise idea of the Irish Dress,—at least of the lay military habit—at this period, I will here transcribe Camden's account of the retinue which attended O'Neal, prince of Ulster, to the court of Elizabeth, A. D. 1562.—" He ap-
"peared at court with his guards of Galloglachs, bare-headed, armed
"with hatchets, their hair flowing in locks on their shoulders, on which
"were yellow surplices dyed with saffron, with long sleeves, short
" coats,

(y) *View of the State of Ireland.*

THE DRESS OF THE IRISH.

"coats (z), and trum jackets, at which ftrange fight, the Londoners "marvelled much."

A learned correfpondent's obfervation on the trum-jackets of O'Neal's attendants is too curious and ingenious to be omitted. " Thrums mean "the unwoven threads which remain to any kind of manufacture that "comes out of the loom; and likewife mean coarfe unwoven yarn: "from which it fhould feem, that thefe jackets were of twifted threads, "and the cords interwoven into, or interlaced with each other, which "may be explained by the paffage relative to the Habergeon of Amadis, "which was deftroyed by the curiofity of thofe who unravelled the "twifted threads thereof."

It is obferved by an eminent French writer, that " une feule eftampe ferait mieux entendre que vingt pages de defcription." Convinced of the juftnefs of this obfervation, and willing to throw on my fubject every light with which my refearches have fupplied me, I fhall here exhibit to your lordfhip a rude, but faithful delineation of O'More, a turbulent Irifh chieftain of this reign, and Archer, a Jefuit retained by him, both copied from A MAP OF THE TAKING OF THE EARL OF ORMOND in 1600 (a), Plate X. fig. 1. 2. preferved amongft the manufcripts

---

(z) From the fhort coats of O'Neal's guards, who were certainly in their military Drefs, it fhould feem, that that refinement of chivalry then prevailed in Ireland, which forbid the ftriking " ailleurs qu'entre les quatres membres."

(a) An engraving of this map (as it is entitled) is given in CAREW's *Pacat. Hib.* but it is by no means faithful. The fidelity of the delineation of the figures here given, (tho' on a large fcale,) may be relied upon: even the original colours of the drawing are preferved.

scripts of our College, and which is said to have been taken on the spot. O'More, fig. 2. is dressed in the barrad and scarlet cloak, and Archer, fig. 1. in the black mantle and strait truise.

Before I dispatch the reign of our virgin Queen, I shall extract from THE CORPORATION-BOOK OF IRISHTOWN (Kilkenny) some sumptuary bye laws touching the dress of the inhabitants of that town in the years 1537, and 1565.

" By an order of the court made by the portrieve, burgesses and commons of Irishtown, 7th Jan. 1537, it was ordered, that the following prices should be paid within the said corporation, for making the underneath particulars, viz.

A quilted dublet, with a new fashioned Bellire *(b)* to be cut, to be made for one shilling sterling.

The pair of Gally-enishes *(c)*, to be made for eight pence.

The pair of new fashioned close hose, six pence *(d)*.

The

(*b*) A learned friend takes Bellire to be an Englishwoman's petticoat.

(*c*) Gally-enich is conjectured by the same friend, to be an Englishman's shirt, short and tight, instead of the Irishman's of thirty ells.

(*d*) This was certainly a liberal price for the making of a pair of hose, as they were probably made of common cloth; for the art of knitting, it is most probable, was now unknown in Ireland, as it does not appear to have been a common art in England or in

any

THE DRESS OF THE IRISH.

The woman's Irish coat, double seamed, being not wrought with silk, seven pence.

Every ounce of silk to be wrought upon a woman's coat, for nine pence.

The offender to forfeit two shillings.

Anno 1565. " A bye law in the corporation of Irishtown : that no inhabitant dwelling within the mitre land, being a free-man, or woman, wear no apparel but after the English fashion; nor no woman wear any caps upon pain of forfeiture; and that every burgess shall go in his cloak, and so every freeman, upon pain of forfeiture, excepting W. Dullany, Teig Lowry, and R. Wale."

Although on the verge, we must not quit this age of credulity without noticing the magic girdles now worn by the Irish. Sir John Harington, one of the brightest ornaments of the court of Elizabeth, in a note on his translation of THE ORLANDO FURIOSO (e), tells us, " that " some say it is a great practise in Ireland to charme girdles, and the like, " perswading men that while they weare them they cannot be hurt with " any

---

any other part of Europe at this period. See SMITH's *Wealth of Nations.* Vol. I. p. 389. In HOLINGSHED's *Chron. of Irel.* we find mention of " strait stockings" under the reign of Henry VIII. p. 89.

(e) Book 12.

"any weapon (*f*)." This he illuſtrates with a little narrative, which, as it preſents us with a picture of the times, in ſimple colouring, I ſhall make no apology for tranſcribing here. " Rorie Oge (a notable rebell " of Ireland) having taken, in a vile and trecherous parlee, my valiant " coſin Sir Henrie Harington priſoner, had one night his cabin or " little hovell where he lay, beſet with one hundred ſouldiers of the ſaid " Sir Henrie his band, meaning to reſcue their captaine by force, ſith the " rebels demaunds for his delivery were ſuch as Sir Henrie himſelfe (be- " ing his priſoner) would not condeſcend unto, but would rather hazard " his life as he knew he ſhould : I ſay theſe hundred men wel appointed, " beſet the houſe ſtrongly, being made of nothing but hardels and durt, " yet the villain, ere they could get in, get up in his ſhirt, and gave the " knight xiiij, wounds very deadly, and after gat thorough them all with- " out hurt, where a mouſe almoſt could not have got betweene them : " and I have heard it affirmed in Ireland, that it was with meere witch- " craft."—It may be preſumed that Rorie, though ſurprized, did not for- get his girdle, and that his miraculous eſcape is ſilently attributed by our author, to its witching powers.

Having eſcaped from the magic circle drawn around us by Sir John Harington, we will now proceed to the reign of James I. which I ſhall open with the coarſe deſcription of the Iriſh Dreſs

given

(*f*) Enchanted girdles were in early uſe in Ireland. Vide *Vind. of Anc. Hiſt. of Ireland*, p. 207. 459.—and in the north of Scotland, till very lately, they were kept in many families. Vide MACPHERSON's *Poems of Oſſian*, p. 125. note. quarto ed. and WHITAKER's *Hiſt. of Manch*. Vol. I. p. 369. In the poem of *Oran eadar Ailte agus Mac-Ronain air dhoibh fearg a ghabhail ri Fionn*, already mentioned, the maid ſent by Fin to offer friend-ſhip to the wrathful Erragon, on his landing in Ireland, enumerates with other gifts, " an hundred girdles" and adds, " ſickneſs cannot affect thoſe whom they bind, they ſtop pain and torture, a grateful preſent to pregnant women." *Tranſ. of the Roy. Iriſh Academy*. Antiq. p. 88.

given by Morryfon, who vifited this kingdom during the period under confideration. " In Ireland the Englifh, and the Englifh-
" Irifh are attired after the Englifh manner, for the moft part, yet not
" with fuch pride and inconftancy, perhaps for want of means: yet the
" Englifh-Irifh forgetting their own country, are fomewhat infected
" with the Irifh rudenefs, and with them are delighted in fimple colours,
" as red and yellow.—Touching the meere or wild Irifh, it may truely
" be faid of them, which of old was fpoken of the Germans, namely,
" that they wander flovenly and naked, and lodge in the fame houfe (if
" it may be called a houfe) with their beafts *(g)*. Among them the
" gentleman or lords of counties weare clofe Breeches and Stockings of
" the fame piece of cloth, or red or fuch light colour, and a loofe coat,
" and a cloak or three cornered Mantle, commonly of coarfe light ftuffe
" made at home, and their linen is coarfe and flovenly. I fay flovenly,
" becaufe they feldom put off a fhirt till it be worn *(h)*: And thofe
" fhirts in our memory, before the laft rebellion, were made of fome
" twenty or thirty elles, folded in wrinkles and coloured with faf-
" fron *(i)*.—Their wives living among the Englifh are attired in a
" fluttifh Gown, to be faftened at the breaft with a lace, and in a more

" fluttifh

(*g*) This feems to juftify the obfervation of DE LOLME, that "the Irifh, from their peculiar cuftoms, their appearance and Drefs, were, in regard to the Englifh, a foreign, we might almoft fay, a remote nation." *Brit. Emp. in Europe*, p. 50.

(*h*) My regard for truth, and my duty as an hiftorian, oblige me to declare, that this flovenly cuftom, fo juftly reprobated by Morryfon, prevailed, at leaft partially, amongft the heads of fome of the principal Irifh families, fo low as the laft reign (Geo. II.)

(*i*) Speaking of the profufion of linen ufed by the Irifh, DE LOLME takes occafion to remark, that, " Ireland feems to have been deftined, from time immemorial, to poffefs a flourifhing linen manufacture. *Brit. Emp. in Europe*, p. 50.

"fluttish Mantell, and more fluttish linen *(k)*; and their heads be co-
"vered after the Turkish manner, with many elles of linen; only the
"Turkish heads or Turbans are round in the top: but the attire of the
"Irish womens heads is more flat in the top and broader in the sides,
"not much unlike a cheese mot, if it had a hole to put in the head *(l)*.
"For the rest, in the remote parts, where the English laws and man-
"ners are unknown, the very chiefs of the Irish as well men as wo-
"men, goe naked in winter time."

This last assertion seems to be, in some degree, corroborated by the following description of the Irish Dress which Sir John Harington has foisted into his translation of THE ORLANDO FURIOSO; though the courteous knight modestly throws a Mantle over the nakedness of our countrymen:

> Then come the Irish men of valiant harts,
> And active limbs, in personages tall,
> They naked use to go in many parts,
> But with a *Mantle* yet they cover all *(m)*.

But

(k) The dress of the female peasant at this time is thus allusively described by ARTHUR WILSON in his *Life of James* I. "In Antwerp they pictured the Queen of Bohemia
"like a poor Irish mantler, with her hair hanging about her ears, and her child at
"back."

(l) On this mode of covering the head, which had probably prevailed time im-memorial in Ireland, a correspondent observes, "the women's ancient head-dress so per-
"fectly resembles that of the Egyptian Isis, that it cannot be doubted but that the modes
"of Egypt were preserved amongst the Irish; the covering of the head with rolls or
"folds of linen, being so noted a mark of the eastern customs, that its source cannot be
"disputed, for there the heat of the sun required that precaution."

(m) Book 10. st. 74. It is not indeed improbable that the Irish while necessitated to be in

constant

THE DRESS OF THE IRISH.

But as this description appears in a work dedicated to Queen Elizabeth its fidelity may be justly questioned. While her Majesty was ruling the Irish with an iron sceptre, a poet who wished to court her smiles would not be so impolitic as to flatter the unhappy sufferers, or to exhibit such a picture of their customs and manners as would be likely to excite commiseration. Even Morryson, as if sensible that his assertion did not rest on the basis of truth, endeavoured to support it with a relation, (rather too indelicate for insertion) of a German baron, who had travelled in Ireland. But Dr. Leland does not seem inclined to give credit either to Morryson, or his friend the baron, and combats their assertions with sound reasoning. " Morryson in his travels (says he) informs us, " that an Irish chieftain, with his family and attendants, sat round " his fire, naked. There is little doubt but that in the reign of Eliza- " beth, even the old natives had degenerated, and that the wars of seve- " ral centuries had reduced them to a state inferior to that in which the " English found them in the days of Henry II. Yet the fact is totally " incredible. The climate of Ireland must at all times have forced the " most barbarous to some covering, even in their retired chambers" *(n)*.

I entirely accord in opinion with Dr. Leland as to the incredibility of Morryson's relation, and am willing to suppose that Speed, a writer

of

constant readiness to take the field, in defence of their property, used every means to render themselves hardy. The author of *The description of Ireland in* HOLINGSHED's *Chronicle*, notices the hardy manner in which the vulgar Irish brought up their children in his time : " their infants, they of meaner sort, are neither swadled nor lapped in linnen, " but folded up starke naked in a blanket till they can go." p. 44.

(*n*) *Hist. of Irel.* Pref. Disc.

of this reign, has kept much clofer to the truth. I fhall therefore give his defcription of the Irifh Drefs, which your lordfhip will find fimple, accurate and curious. " Their wives were many, by reafon of
" divorcements, and their maids at twelve yeeres of age, whofe
" cuftomes were to fend to their lovers, Bracelets plaited and curioufly
" wrote (wrought) of their own haire *(o)*, fo farre following Venus
" in the knots of their allurements *(p)*. The men wore linen Shirts
" exceedingly large, ftained with faffron, the fleeves wide, and hanging
" to their knees, ftrait and fhort Truffes plaited thick in the fkirts, their
" Breeches clofe to the thighs, a fhort Skeine hanging point down
" before, and Mantle moft times caft over their heads. The women
" wore their haire plaited in curious manner, hanging down their backs
" and fhoulders from under folden wreathes of fine linen, rolled about
" their heads, rather loading the wearer than delighting the beholder : for
" as the one was moft feemely, fo the other was unfightly : their neckes
" were hung with Chains and Carkanets, their arms wreathed with many
" Bracelets, and over their fide garments the fhagge rugge Mantles
" purfled

(o) In *The Annals of Ulfter* we find mention, under the year 1004, of Bracelets ; but they were probably of more intrinfic value than thofe fent to their lovers by the Irifh ladies, in the time of Speed, for they appear to have been given, together with 60 oz. of gold, and a golden cup, to purchafe the ranfom of a captive King.—Of a Soilfeach or amulet in the form of a bracelet, and which was probably worn as fuch, an engraving is given in *Collect. de Reb. Hib.* No. XIII. Plate XIV. fig. 1.

(p) By " knots of allurements" Speed evidently alludes to the truelove knot, the ancient fymbol of love, faith and friendfhip among the Northern nations. Vide BRAND's *Obf. on Pop. Antiq.* p. 349.

THE DRESS OF THE IRISH.

" purfled *(p)* with a deep fringe of divers colours, both fexes account-
" ing idleneffe their only libertie, and eaffe their greateft riches *(q)*.

However it was in this reign, (James I.) that the Irifh Drefs was to feel the influence of fafhion, and to affume a new form. The circuits of the judges being now no longer confined within the narrow limits of the pale, but embracing the whole kingdom, the civil affemblies at the affizes and feffions, (fays Sir John Davies) reclaimed the Irifh from their wildnefs; caufed them to cut off their glibs and long hair; to convert their mantles into cloaks; and to conform themfelves to the manner of England in all their behaviour and outward forms (*r*).

But this reformation was not occafioned by the influence of fafhion alone; the civil power afforded its wholefome aid. The lord deputy Chichefter in his inftructions for the lord prefident and council of Munfter, 20th May 1615, directs, that " to the end a comely and decent
" order may be obferved by the fheriffs, juftices of peace, jurors, and
" other officers of juftice, freeholders and others, in all feffions and
" fitting terms, that the faid lord deputy and council do think it conve-
" nient, that the faid lord prefident and council there, by their procla-
" mation or otherwife, give ftraight order, that all the faid perfons,
" in

(*p*) Purfled. From the Fr. Pourflier, which properly fignifies to work upon the edge. TYRWHITT, *Cant. Tales*, Vol. IV. p. 199.—Embroidered. PERCY, Glofs. to *Reliques*.

(*q*) *Theat. of the Emp. of Great Brit.*—In SPEED's map of the four principal cities of Ireland, he has given engravings of the Dreffes of the country.

(*r*) *Difc.* p. 215. oct. ed.

"in all times of seffions and fitting terms, do ufe and wear Englifh "attire and apparel; punifhing by fine and imprifonment all fuch as "fhall appear before them attired in Mantles and Robes, and punifh "the wearer; and alfo to expel and cut all Glibs" (s).

Admitting that thofe inftructions were religioufly obferved, we may hence conclude, that the Irifh gentlemen now began to figure in Cloaks, Ruffs, and fometimes Troufers; and often indulged in the vanity of yellow ftockings, filk garters puffed in a large knot below the knees, and knots and rofes in their fhoes. For fuch was the Drefs of the Englifh at this period (t). It is probable too, that at this time, Hats were firft introduced into Ireland; for it is rather a matter of doubt, that they were worn in England before the reign of Elizabeth (u). Indeed if we may credit a fcholiaft on Cambrenfis' account of THE CONQUEST OF IRELAND, the Irifh had no need of hats whilft they cherifhed their hair. "The Irifh nation and people even from the beginning "(fays my author) have been alwaies of a hard bringing up, and are "not onelie rude in apparell, but alfo rough and ouglie in their bodies: "their beards and heads they never wafh, clenfe, nor cut, efpeciallie "their heads; the haire whereof they fuffer to grow, faving that fome "doo ufe to round it: and by reafon the fame is never kembed, it grow- "eth faft togither, and in proceffe of time it matteth fo thicke and

faft

(s) *Defid. Curiofa Hibern.* Vol. II. p. 20.

(t) GRANGER's *Biog. Hift. of Eng.* Vol. II. p. 319. quarto ed. This is precifely the Spanifh mode of Drefs, which I fuppofe was introduced into England by Philip, confort of Queen Mary.

(u) Ibid. Vol. I. p. 163.

" faft togither, that it is, *infteed of a hat*, and keepeth the head verie
" warme, and alfo will beare off a great blow or ftroke (*x*), and this
" head of haire they call a glibe, and therein they have a great plea-
" fure" (*y*).

With refpect to the drefs of the Irifh ladies in this reign, I can only conjecture, that, like the Englifh women, they began to opprefs their heads with ornaments, and to court the amorous glance by expofing their bofoms (*z*).

The Drefs of the nobility in the next reign (Charles I.) may be in part collected from the following refolution of the houfe of commons, A. D. 1644.

" That the houfe gave no direction to Ridgely Hatfield, nor to any
" other, for taking into their hands, or cuftody, and goods of the right
" honourable the lord baron of Dunfany; and do think fit and fo order,
" that

(*x*) In *The Coxcomb* of BEAUMONT and FLETCHER, Maria calls Antonio, while in the difguife of an Irifh footman, " firrah thatch'd head," in allufion, I prefume, to the matted appearance of his hair, intended to render his difguife the more compleat.

(*y*) HOLINGSHED's *Chronicle*.

(*z*) To the fhame of modern Europe, this indecent cuftom, which, within my own memory, prevailed amongft my country-women, was ftrictly prohibited amongft the unenlightened Gentoos. Vide *A Code of Gentoo Laws*. Ch. 20.

" that the said Hatfield do forthwith deliver unto his lordship, the
" goods in the schedule, to his lordship's petition annexed, specified,
" viz. two broad clothe cloaks of black, the bayes of one of them lose;
" two black clothe cashokes; one riding black cloth coat, faced
" with plush; one black gown of plush for a man, lined with baize;
" two yards and an half of black broad cloth, and a pair of black
" boot hose tops of cloth lined with taffety, taking his lordship's note
" for receipt of those goods" (a).

But we are not to presume that the Irish nobility and gentry in general dressed after the mode of my lord Dunsany. In order then to give your lordship some idea of the most prevalent fashion of Dress amongst the higher classes of the Irish at this time, I shall take leave to direct your lordship's notice to some figures on the superb tomb of Sir Gerald Aylmer and his dame, Julia Nugent, at Donadea, in the county of Kildare, Plate XI. fig. 1. 2. I do not however, mean to infer, that Sir Gerald and his dame led the fashions; at least I do not think they did so at court; there I conclude every body was dressed in the English style, and there we are taught to believe the dresses were splendid. James Howell, a writer of this reign, in a letter from Dublin, dated 3d May 1639, says, " Here is a most splendid court kept at the Castle, and ex-
" cept that of the vice-roy of Naples, I have not seen the like in Chris-
" tendom"

(a) *Journ. of the House of Comm.* App. p. 170. Belts or Girdles continued so low as this time to be worn by the Irish. It appeared on the examination of Mr. Lambert before the Irish house of commons, A. D. 1641, for ill-treatment of Mr. Johnson, that he had pulled him (Johnson) by the *belt*, and hawled him about the street. Ibid. p. 52.

THE DRESS OF THE IRISH.

" tendom (*b*)." Now, as it is not probable that the splendour to which our author alludes could have proceeded solely from the decorations of the court, it may be safely concluded that the dresses of those by whom it was frequented, must have joined in exciting his admiration.

Before I dismiss the pious and unfortunate Charles, I must do him the justice to declare, that by an act passed at Dublin, in the 10th year of his reign, " FOR REPEALE OF DIVERS STATUTES HERETOFORE " ENACTED IN THIS KINGDOM OF IRELAND" (*c*), he permitted the Beard to flourish once more on the upper lip of our countrymen, privileged them to use again gilt Bridles, Peytrels, and other gilt Harneys, and left them at liberty to wear either their own national dress or the English apparel. All this however was done, say the framers of the act, because those Statutes " are now by reason of the blessed change of " times, grown out of use, and many of them not fit to be continued, " as not sorting with the condition of the present times, and the happy " government under which the subjects of this kingdom doe live. " And that after so long a quiet among his Majesties subjects thereof, " whose zeale to his Majesties service is manifested upon all occasions,

" any

(*b*) *Epistolæ Ho-Elianæ*, p. 274. For the manner in which the State officers were attired at this time on state-days, Vide *Desid. Cur. Hib.* Vol. 1. p. 166.

(*c*) It must however be admitted that the trade of Ireland has great obligations to Charles. Under his auspices several valuable manufactures were planted and encouraged in different parts of the kingdom; particularly at Chapelizod, Clonmell, and Dundalk. See LAWRENCE's *Int. of Ireland.* p. 188, 189.

" any national diſtinction or difference between them, might prove dan-
" gerous."

The ſword of rebellion having drank to ſatiety of the blood of the proteſtants, and the ruins of the eſtabliſhed church being again repaired, the banners of peace waved once more o'er our enſanguined fields, and a friendly intercourſe began to ſubſiſt between the Engliſh and the Iriſh. United now in the bands of friendſhip, both nations aſſumed the ſame garb: but Faſhion continued to hold her throne in England (*d*). Hence I conclude—and the voice of tradition ſupports me—that open-ſleeves, pantaloons, ſhoulder knots, Flanders-lace, neck-clothes (*e*), and that moſt ridiculous of all faſhions, the Perriwig (*f*), were worn by the Iriſh nobility and gentry at this period; and that the ladies began to curl and frizzle their hair. But wanting the information of portraits, I cannot deſcend into all the minutiæ of the dreſs of thoſe times. I can indeed deſcribe a Fan that was then worn by one of our country women, for it now lies before me. The mount is a thin kind of ſilk; the ground deep blue, and the figures fanciful and rude. The ſticks are of ivory ſtained brown; thoſe on the

outſide

(*d*) Now, and for ſome time before, the Romiſh clergy went about exhorting the people to throw off the Mantle and Trouſe; but their exhortations were of little avail.

(*e*) That Flanders-lace ſoon found its way into Ireland, appears from the following anecdote in a letter of Mr. O'HALLORAN. "The late lord Glandore told me, that when a boy, under a ſpacious tomb at his ſeat near Ardfert, he perceived ſomething white. He drew it forth; and it proved to be a ſhroud of Flanders-lace, the covering of a perſon long ſince deceaſed."

(*f*) It is little to the credit of this unſeemly covering of the head, that the firſt perſon recorded to have worn a wig in England, was Saxton, fool to Henry VIII. WALPOLE's *Anec. of Paint.* Vol. I. p. 135.

outside covered with elegant silver filigreen work, and studded with amethysts (*g*).

According to Harris, about this time the Mantle and Trouse began to fall into disuse amongst the Irish peasantry. "Lieutenant colonel "Humphry Hurd (says he) deputy governor of Galway, in the ab- "sence of colonel Peter Stubbers who governed that garrison under the "usurpers, issued an order, grounded on the Statute of Henry VIII. "to prohibit the wearing of the Mantle to all people whatsoever; "which was executed with great rigour, and from that time the Mantle "and Trowse were disused for the most part (*h*)." And Sir Henry Piers, in his DESCRIPTION OF THE COUNTY OF WESTMEATH written in this reign, tells us, that "there is now no more appearance of "the Irish Cap, Mantle, or Trowses, at least in these countries."

It appears from THE POLITICAL ANATOMY OF IRELAND by that keen observer, Sir William Petty, that those articles of Dress thus prohibited but not generally disused, were then (1672) made of a narrow sort of frize, of that kind perhaps which was exempted from alnage by a particular Statute in 8th Edw. III. (*i*). "The cloathing
(says

(*g*) Mr. O'HALLORAN assures us, that within his memory amethysts of immense value were found in Ireland. *Introd. to Hist. and Antiq. of Irel.* p. 116.

(*h*) WARE's *Works*, Vol. II. p. 177. In act 2. of *The Coxcomb* of BEAUMONT and FLETCHER, there is a very indelicate but witty allusion to the immoderate size of the Trouse under the name of Dousets.

(*i*) ANDERSON's *Hist. of Comm.* Vol. I. p. 204.

" (fays my author, fpeaking of the Irifh) is a narrow fort of frieze, of
" about twenty inches broad, whereof two foot, call'd a bandle, is
" worth from 3½d. to 18d. Of this, feventeen bandles make a man's
" fuit, and twelve make a cloak (k)." In another part of the fame work he gives us the current prices, at that time, of feveral articles of Drefs in ufe amongft the vulgar. " They wear (fays he) fuch cloaths
" as the wool of their own fheep, fpun into yarn by themfelves, doth
" make; their fhoes, called brogues, are but $\frac{1}{4}$ fo much worth as a pair
" of Englifh fhoes; nor of more than $\frac{1}{2}$ in real ufe and value.
" A hat cofts 20d. a pair of ftockings 6d. but a good fhirt near
" 3s (l)."

As we have no reafon to fufpect Sir William Petty on this occafion of mifreprefentation, we may prefume, that his obfervation was confined to the peafantry. For Richard Lawrence, in his INTEREST OF IRELAND, publifhed in 1682, tells us, in an angry tone, that tradefmen's wives wear not only filk gowns, but oft-times two or three filk petticoats; and reprobates the general ufe of filk hoods and fcarfs amongft even the inferior claffes of the people (m). To this he attributes, amongft other caufes, the decay of trade and wealth in Ireland at that time; and prophetically declares, that " if poor Ireland imi-
" tates rich England in garb, it will be beggared."

(k) P. 98.
(l) Ibid. p. 76.
(m) P. 20.

THE DRESS OF THE IRISH.

Of the dreſſes of the turbulent reign of James II. I cannot ſpeak with certainty; for little is certainly known. If any particular faſhion prevailed at that time, it was probably of Engliſh origin. Some of the female peaſantry, however, ſtill continued attached to their old habits. Of theſe I will here deſcribe one, as worn to the hour of her death by Mary Morgan, a poor woman, who was married before the battle of the Boyne, and lived to the year 1786.—On her head ſhe wore a roll of linen, not unlike that on which milk-maids carry their pails, but with this difference, that it was higher behind than before; over this ſhe combed her hair, and covered the whole with a little round-eared cap, or coif, with a border ſewed on plain;—over all this was thrown a kerchief, which, in her youth, was made faſt on the top of her head, and let to fall careleſly behind; in her old age it was pinned under her chin.—Her jacket was of brown cloth, or preſſed frize, and made to fit cloſe to the ſhape by means of whale-bone wrought into it before and behind; this was laced in front, but not ſo as to meet, and through the lacing were drawn the ends of her neck-kerchief. The ſleeves, halfway to the elbows, were made of the ſame kind of cloth with the jacket; thence continued to the wriſt of red chamlet ſtriped with green ferreting; and there, being turned up, formed a little cuff embraced with three circles of green riband. Her petticoat was invariably of either ſcarlet frize or cloth, bordered with three rows of green riband. Her apron green ſerge, ſtriped longitudinally with ſcarlet ferreting, and bound with the ſame. Her hoſe were blue worſted. And her ſhoes of black leather, faſtened with thongs, or ſtrings.

This faſhion of habit however, had not been always peculiar to the peaſantry: it appears to have prevailed formerly in the principal Iriſh families.

families. About the close of the last century, there lived at Credan, near Waterford, a Mrs. Power, a lady of considerable fortune, who, as being lineally descended from some of the Kings of Munster, was vulgarly called, The Queen of Credan. This lady, proud of her country and descent, always spoke the Irish language, and affected the Dress and manners of the ancient Irish. Her Dress, in point of fashion, answered exactly to that of Mary Morgan as just described; but was made of richer materials. The border of her coif was of the finest Brussels-lace; her kerchief of clear muslin; her jacket of the finest brown cloth, trimmed with narrow gold lace, and the sleeves of crimson velvet striped with the same; and her petticoat of the finest scarlet cloth, bordered with two rows of broad gold lace.

The Hugonots who followed the fortunes of William III. brought with them the fashions of their county. But I cannot find that these fashions were infectious; at least it does not appear that the Irish caught them.

The Hat was now shaped in the Ramillie cock. The Perriwig, which had been of several years standing in Ireland, was not yet generally worn: it was confined to the learned professions, or to those who affected gravity. " Our ignorant nation (says Farquhar, in a comedy written in this reign) our ignorant nation imagine, a *full wig* as infallible " a token of wit as the laurel (*n*)."

The head-dress, which the Spectator says, " made the women of " such an enormous stature, that we appeared as grass-hoppers before " them," now prevailed here. This information I owe to the inquisitiveness of Lucinda, in the comedy which I have just quoted.

Lucinda.

(*n*) *Love and a Bottle.* Act 1.

Lucinda. Tell us some news of your country; I have heard the strangest stories,—that the people wear horns and hoofs.

Roebuck.—Yes faith, a great many wear horns; but we have that, among other laudable fashions, from London; I think it came over with your mode of wearing *high top knots*; for ever since, the men and wives bear their heads *exalted alike*. They were both fashions that took wonderfully.

The reign of Queen Anne seems to have been an age of gay attire *(o)*: the single Dress of a woman of quality then, was the product of an hundred climes *(p)*. Swift, in a poem written in 1708, thus metamorphoses the Dress of his Goody Baucis into the Dress of the day.

> Instead of home-spun *Coifs*, were seen
> Good *pinners* edg'd with *Colberteen*,
> Her petticoat transform'd apace,
> Became *black sattin* flounc'd with *lace*.

(o) Even the Dress of the dead was attended to in this reign. We learn from *The Journals of the House of Commons*, that a bill was brought into parliament in 1703, and afterwards passed into a law, to oblige all persons in this kingdom to bury in woollen. This was probably done in conformity to the English custom, to which Pope alludes in his *Moral Essays*, Ep. 1. v. 245.

Odious! in woollen! t'would a saint provoke, &c.

(p) *Spectator*, No. 69.

Plain Goody would no longer down,
'Twas Madam in her *Grogram* gown (*q*).

Besides the different articles of Dress enumerated in those lines, the Irish ladies wore short jackets with close sleeves, made of Spanish cloth, each side of which was dyed of a different colour: These jackets were fastened on the breast with ribands. Their petticoats were swelled to so monstrous a circumference by means of hoops, as must have alarmed the opposite sex for their chastity. High stays, piked before and behind, gave an awkward stiffness to their carriage. Their shoes were of red and blue Spanish leather, laced with broad gold and silver lace at top and behind; the heels broad, and of a moderate height: some were fastened with silver clasps, others with knots or roses. Their stockings were generally of blue or scarlet worsted or silk, ornamented with clocks worked with gold or silver thread (*r*): neither thread nor cotton hose were then known. And their necks were usually adorned with black collars, tied in front, with ribands of divers colours.

I cannot find that the riding coat, in such general use amongst the English ladies in this reign, and so justly reprobated by the Spectator (*s*),

was

(*q*) *Baucis and Philemon.*

(*r*) Scarlet stockings were worn by the English ladies also at this time. ADDISON alludes to this fashion with his usual humour, in the bill of Mortality prefixed to a paper in the *Spectator* on the effects of love, (No. 377. May 13, 1712). " T. S. wounded by " Zelinda's *scarlet stockings*, as she was stepping out of a coach."

(*s*) No. 104. 435. But tho' the ladies did not wear riding-coats, it is probable that they wore buskins when on horseback; for I not only find this article under the head of
" Inwards,"

THE DRESS OF THE IRISH.

was now worn here: Dress had not yet mingled the sexes. A lady, in those days, mounted her horse in the same dress in which she entered the drawing-room;—nay, she did not even forget her hoop.

" There is not, (says Addison) so variable a thing in nature as a lady's head-dress (*t*)". The justness of this observation deters me from attempting to describe the head-dress of the ladies of those days. I shall be content with concluding, that it rose and fell with the head-dress of the English ladies; which, within Addison's memory, rose and fell above thirty degrees (*u*). I must however observe, that I cannot learn, on the strictest enquiry, that the lovely tresses of nature were then permitted, as in the present day*, to wanton on the neck, where (to borrow the language of Hogarth) " the many waving and contrasted " turns of naturally intermingling locks, ravish the eye with the plea- " sure of the pursuit, especially when put in motion by a gentle " breeze (*v*)."

But though I wave any attempt to describe the fashion of the ladies' hair at that time, I ought not to omit to mention, that they wore

Hoods

" Inwards," in a *Book of Rates* published by CH. YOUNG in 1702, but recollect having been once told by an old lady, that in her youth, the ladies always rode in buskins.

(*t*) *Spect.* No. 98.

(*u*) Ibid.

(*) This late improvement of my fair country-women in their ideas of natural elegance in hair-dressing, was probably suggested by the works of Angelica, Reynolds, &c. an effect which the author of *A Treatise on Hair-dressing*, wonders was not sooner produced.

(*v*) *Anal. of Beauty*, p. 28.

Hoods of divers colours (*w*), and beaver Hats trimmed with broad gold and silver lace, and a buckle in front.

Wafted by the breath of fashion, the Mask alighted in this island (*x*). Immediately the ladies took it up, and appeared in it in the streets, public walks and theatres. Under this disguise, they could now, without fear of discovery, rally their lovers or their friends, and safely smile at the obscenity of a comedy (*y*). Patches too were much worn: but whether or not their position was determined, as in England, by the spirit of party, I cannot say (*z*).

I have been informed that some Irish ladies of this reign, affected the Dress in which the unfortunate Queen of Scots is usually depicted. So that we may presume the Ruff now occasionally rose about the neck of our lovely countrywomen.

The Dress of the gentlemen in this reign, was more uniform than that of the ladies. Their coats and waistcoats were laced with broad gold

(*w*) The practice of wearing hoods, was borrowed from the English, amongst whom we find they were in use so early as the reign of Hen. VIII. from an act passed in England in the 33d. year of that reign. We also find them mentioned in a ballad of the reign of Elizabeth. PERCY's *Reliq.* Vol. 1. p. 309.

(*x*) These masks were made of velvet and sattin, and imported at an high duty. Vide YOUNG's *Collect. of several Acts and Stat. relating to the Rev. of Irel.* p. 59.

(*y*) Masks continued to be worn by some of our countrywomen so late as the reign of Geo. II.—About forty years since, a lady of distinction was seen to go hunting in a Mask with the late Mr. Conolly, from his lodge at Mount-Venus.

(*z*) *Spect.* No. 43.

THE DRESS OF THE IRISH.

gold or silver lace: the skirts of each were long, and the sleeves of the coat slashed. Instead of stocks, they wore cravats, edged with Flanders or Brussels-lace, which, after passing several times round the neck, wandered through the button holes of the coat, almost the whole length of the body. Their hose, like those of the ladies, were blue or scarlet worsted or silk, worked with gold or silver clocks. Their shoes, in this (and in the following reign) had broad square toes, short quarters and high tops; and were made fast with small buckles (*a*). Their heads,—even the heads of youthful beaux—were enveloped in monstrous perriwigs (*b*), on which perched a small felt hat. And thro' the skirts of their coats stiffened with buckram, peeped the hilt of a small sword.

Long cloaks too of Spanish cloth, each side dyed of a different colour, were now worn by the gentlemen (*c*).

With

(*a*) When shoe-buckles were first introduced into this kingdom by the English, I have not been able to learn. That they were in use in England in the reign of Edw. IV. appears from the curious *Collection of Letters of the Paston family*, lately published by Sir JOHN FENN. Vol. II. p. 203.

(*b*) Almost all the portraits of military commanders of this reign that I have seen, are dressed in armour and enormous perriwigs.

(*c*) This fashion, inter alia, was derived from our neighbours in Great Britain, amongst whom, however, it had fallen into disuse about this time. In the reign of Philip and Mary, the companions of the Inns of Court were forbid by one of their regulations, to wear Spanish gowns in common. REEVE's *Hist. of the Eng. Law.* Vol. IV. p. 574. oct. ed.

With the line of the Stuarts, I shall close this crude Essay. For, from the accession of George I. to the present day, Fashion has been such a varying goddess in this country, that neither history, tradition nor painting, has been able to preserve all her mimic forms: like Proteus struggling in the arms of Telemachus on the Pharian coast, she passed from shape to shape with the rapidity of thought.

But your lordship, I fear, will think I have dwelt too long on so trifling a subject. I must confess, that Dress, in the general acceptation of the word, is a subject of little importance; but the national Dress of our ancestors receives some consequence from the circumstance of its having been so often the object of parliamentary consideration. Indeed the history of the Dress of any nation does, in some degree, involve that of the manners of its inhabitants: it is a mirror in which we can discern the progress of society; at one time we may see her falling into the depths of barbarism, and again emerging into the light of civilization. When we behold the Irish wrapped in skins, or concealing a naked form under a coarse woollen mantle, we naturally conclude that we are looking on a race of barbarians; but when we see the same people, in other periods, clad in silk, fringed with gold or silver lace, and their persons glittering with elegant and costly ornaments, we cannot deny them the respect which is due to a wealthy and a civilized, if not a polished people.

From the history of the Irish Dress it may also be observed, that the English, for many centuries after they had invaded this island, used oppressive and unwarrantable measures to bring the natives into subjection: under the specious pretext of civilizing them, they compelled them

THE DRESS OF THE IRISH.

them into a conformity of dress and manners, only the more easily to bow their heads to the yoke.

It must, however, be confessed that while the Irish retained their uncouth and barbarous Dress (for such it appears to have been in latter times) their laws and their language, little could be effected towards the introduction of modern refinement amongst them. This consideration alone, seems for the two last centuries, to have actuated the English government in the ordaining sumptuary laws in this kingdom. Nor can we deny, that from the reign of Elizabeth, the English, instead of denuding the natives with the rude hand of power, used gentle means to induce them to lay aside their national Dress, and to assimilate with themselves in customs and habits. The happy consequences of of these measures we now experience, and are bound in gratitude to kiss the rod which formerly chastised our ancestors. What your lordship has done towards effectuating our present political happiness, delicacy forbids me to mention. Future pens will record it.

Having thus sketched the outlines of this, I hope, not uninteresting or incurious subject, I trust some abler hand may be found to lay in the colouring, and finish the picture. And in this hope I freely abandon it.

I have the honor to be,

My Lord,

with profound respect,

your Lordship's

much obliged,

and most obedient humble servant,

Joseph Cooper Walker.

Treasury-Chambers,
Dublin,
December 14, 1787.

ADDITIONAL NOTES.

Page 3. Note (*d*) The Celtic Braccæ, fays Mr. Whitaker, &c.

AS the whole paffage is curious and pertinent, I fhall make no apology for tranfcribing it at full length. " The Celtic Braccæ and the Englifh Breeches were fo de-
" nominated from the colours upon them running in ftripes or divifions. And the pre-
" fent trowfers are the original garment a little altered. In its firft ftate it hung
" down to the ancles, entire and undivided, as the petticoats of the women do at pre-
" fent; and is ftill worne in this form by our Blue-coat boys at Manchefter. And the
" next improvement was to open it before, for the greater conveniency of walking; as
" has been practifed with the gowns of fcholars, academicks, and clergymen, and with
" the furplices of the laft very lately; and it is ufed in this ftate by the Bridewell boys
" of London, and our failors. In the original difpofition of the Drefs, therefore, it could
" not be denominated, as might be imagined at firft, from the divifion in its form, but
" was called from the breaks in its colours. *Hift. of Manch.* Vol. II. p. 267.

P. 4. Line 1. The Cota, &c.

Formerly in Gaul, in Ireland and the Highlands of Scotland no raiment was worn below the Cota. Partial to this mode of Drefs, fo well calculated for the free exercife of martial duties, the Highlanders, who ferve on the Britifh eftablifhment, ftill retain it with very little variation. Sir Henry Erskine alludes to this garb in his *Verses addressed to the Royal Highland regiment*:

> With the garb of old Gaul and the fire of old Rome,
> From the heath-cover'd mountains of Scotia we come;
> From the mountains where Romans attempted to reign,
> But our ancestors fought,—and they fought not in vain.
> Tho' no cities nor courts of our habit approve,
> 'Twas presented by Mars at a synod of Jove;
> And when Pallas observ'd at a ball 'twould look odd,
> Mars received from his Venus a smile and a nod.

P. 5. Line 7. Several of the latter instruments (i. e. Dealg-Fallainne,) &c.

On turning over the *Minute-book* of the Committee of Antiq. of the Royal Irish Academy, I found the following memorandums.—

" 1786. Feb. 28. A remarkable silver fibula, similar to that which is deposited in the College Museum, was exhibited to the Committee. It was found near Penrith."—See Plate II. fig. 1.

" June 19. A copper buckle found in the bog of Rosconnel in the Queen's county, was exhibited by the Secretary.—It seemed decidedly to be a buckle, and from its general likeness to the large silver ornament exhibited to the Committee on the 28th Feb. should prove that also to have been designed for the same purpose."

P. 10. Line 5. The Shoe in one form or another, &c.

In the reign of Henry II. slippers were an article of the Dress of the Irish ecclesiastics.—1181. The grant to Wm. Brun was renewed at the rent of forty pence, payable annually at the altar of this church, (Christ-church, Dublin) with certain *Slippers* for the use of the prior." *Monast. Hib.* p. 151.

P. 10.

ADDITIONAL NOTES.

P. 10. Line 13. *The ancient Irish also wore a kind of Buskin, &c.*

The fresco figures at Knockmoy wear a kind of Buskin. Buskins too are worn by the figure of the Bag-piper in the illumination of Dr. Archer's copy of KEATING's *Hist. of Ireland*, already noticed. P. 7.

P. 12. Line 19. *I am inclined to consider the Aiccde, as a kind of Broche, from the circumstance of its marking the rank of the wearer by its value, as was formerly the case amongst the Highlanders, &c.*

Having consulted Mr. Gillies of Perth (the ingenious editor of a collection of *Gaelic Poems* published in 1786,) concerning the ancient Dress of the Caledonians, which is said to have borne so close a resemblance to that of the early Irish, he informed me, inter alia, that Fibulæ or Broches were formerly in frequent use amongst the Highlanders, and that they have not yet laid them aside. " I some time ago (says he) published the " Norwegian *Account of Haco's expedition against Scotland*, translated from the Icelan- " dic, in which mention is made of the conquest of Bute, by a Danish Bard. His " words are, ' the wide extended Bute was won from the forlorn wearers of rings (i. e. the ' Scotch) by the victorious conqueror of conquests.' " In a note at the foot it is observed, " that this was very descriptive of the Highlanders at this period. For we find (he con- " tinues) that the lower rank of them, both men and women, are to a degree fond of " such ornaments. And there is nothing more common in the Highlands of Scotland, " than for beggars, male and female, to fasten their plaids with large silver Felachs or " Broches, that in case of sudden death, they may have as much in value about them as " may be sufficient to defray the expence of their funeral. Golden Broches were very " common in ancient times, and it was only by such ornaments that King's and chiefs " were distinguished from their vassals." Thus it was in Ireland during the Heathen times, with this difference, that the value of the Bodkin or Broche of each class was ascertained by the Brehon Laws. (See above p. 19). I shall here observe, en passant, that one of the charges brought against the Bards in the convention of Drom-Chille, was their having demanded the Broche of the then Monarch. *Hist. Mem. of the Irish Bards.* P. 53.

P. 22.

P. 22. Line 2. Set a due value even on the productions of the needle, &c.

To such perfection were the productions of the needle brought in Ireland in the year 1742, that the Dublin Society gave Robert Baker of Bolton-street, Dublin, a premium of ten pounds, for his art of imitating Brussels lace in needle-work.

P. 22. Line 8. Several golden crowns, &c.

It is a well known fact that the golden crown of a certain fallen family, that formerly ruled over a considerable part of Ireland, was very lately extant.— It is with pain I add, that the necessities of the possessor compelled him to convert this crown, the pride of his family, into money.

P. 27. Note (*m*). Line 5. At this day the peasantry of Connaught and Munster (where the primitive customs and manners still prevail) are clad, &c.

As the estate of my ingenious friend, RICHARD GEOGHEGAN, esq; author of the *Utilitist*, &c. lies in Connaught, I begged of him to favour me with his observations on the prevailing Dress of that province. Though he writes with sportive humour, his letter contains information of too much value to be suppressed. " The dress, or rather the slovenly
" un-dress of the Irish peasantry is but too notorious; and every enquiry about their ap-
" parel must serve only to expose their *nakedness*. Long blue mantles, in the Spanish
" stile *(a)*, bare feet, awkward *Binnogues* or kerchiefs on their heads (generally spotted
" with soot), and madder-red petticoats were and are the prevalent taste of the *Ladies*.
" I have heard my father say, that he remembered some male peasants to wear a *Truifs* or
" piece of knit apparel that served for breeches and stockings; a *Barraid* or scull-cap made
" of ordinary rags, was the ornament of the head; an hatted-man was deemed a Saf-
" fanagh (Saxon) beau. *Brogue-uirleaker*, that is, Flatts made of untanned leather, graced
" their feet, and stockings were deemed a foppery—ought not the modern Irish rather
" draw

(*a*) As the Spaniards frequently landed on the western coasts of this kingdom, it may be presumed, that their national dress was in some instances adopted by the natives.

" draw a veil over such nastiness!—Long beards, bushy hair, and long loose uniformly
" yellowish (not yellow) gowns, and the *Middogues* or dirks, were the principal robes of
" the Irish chieftains, who had an early conference with the English invaders, and being
" laughed at by the latter, a war ensued. This is told I think by Leland, as an historical
" fact."

This letter, although evidently written with a view rather to excite a smile than to inform, serves to corroborate several facts adduced in the foregoing Essay.

P. 29. Line 17. They laid aside their Girdles, their Skeans, &c.

Though girdles were equally worn by all the Celtic nations to fasten their mantles or sacks, *Hist. of Munch.* Vol. 1. p. 228. yet it may be presumed, that the girdles laid aside by the Irish Kings as an earnest of their obedience, were those with which they had been invested on their being created knights. MALMS. B. 2. Ch. 6. For we learn from FROISSART, that the antiquity of knighthood amongst the Irish princes was much higher than the English invasion.—The young Scotch knight, called Ferash, who signalized himself in the defence of his country against the forces of Haco, wore a beautiful belt, of which he was stripped by the Norwegians soon as he fell. See JOHNSTON's Transl. of the Norw. *Acc. of Hacos' exped. against Scotland*, p. 99.

In a translation (now in my possession) of a precious fragment of Icelandic history of the tenth century, entitled *A voyage to Ireland from Iceland*, I find mention of the skean and girdle. An Irish princess resident in Iceland, presents to her son, on the eve of his departure for Ireland, a knife and girdle, which she charges him to deliver to her nurse. The original of this fragment (which has not yet seen the light) is in the valuable collection of lord RAWDON a young nobleman, whose romantic success in arms, can only be equalled by his success in the cultivation of every branch of polite literature.

P. 31. Note *(u)*. This country so remarkably favourable to the linen manufacture, has not been less so to the woollen, &c.

The value of wool in Ireland in the year 1247, is ascertained by the *Regestry* of the priory of the Holy Trinity, Dublin, to have been twenty pence a stone.

P. 31. Note *(v)*. Col. Vallancey gives an high antiquity to the use of rings in Ireland, &c.

In the tranflation from the Icelandic fragment juft quoted, the Irifh princefs alfo prefents to her fon a Ring, faying, " my father made a prefent of this *gold ring* to me on the ap-
" pearance of my firft tooth, and I hope that he will know it again."

P. 40. Line 1. But the ufe of the Glove, &c.

In Ireland, as well as in England, we find gloves enumerated as part of the yearly value given for ancient tenures.—" 1258, Alexander Noke furrendered to the prior (of the " Priory of the Holy Trinity, Dublin) this year the lot of ground that he held from " him in Gilmaholmog-ftreet, near the church of St. Michael, and for which the prior " engaged to pay him yearly two fhillings and *a pair of gloves*, or, in lieu thereof, one " penny." *Monaft. Hib.* p. 160.—It is ftill a prevailing cuftom in Ireland, for the high-fheriff of a county to prefent the juftice of affize with a pair of embroidered or fringed gloves, when the affizes prove maiden. I have not been able to difcover the antiquity or origin of this cuftom.—I fhall now difmifs the fubject of this note with the following curious anecdote from a morning paper of the year 1746. " Yefterday ended at Mr. Langfords in Covent-garden, the fale of the late earl of Arran's curiofities; when the gloves given by Henry VIII. to fir A. Denny, were fold for £38. 17s.—the mittens given by Queen Elizabeth to fir. Edw. Denny's lady, for £25. 4s.—the gloves given by James I. to Ed. Denny, efq; (fon of fir A. Denny) for £22. 1s.—and the fcarf given by Charles I. for £10. 10s. All of which were bought for fir Th. Denny of Ireland, who is lineally defcended from the faid fir A. Denny, one of the executors of Henry VIII."

P. 54. Line 2. Being clofe hooded over his head, &c.

Hooded-men I think are mentioned fomewhere in the Irifh Statutes under the defcription of Affaffins.

P. 54.

P. 54. Note (*u*). Made of rug, &c.

In the time of James I. the best rugs were manufactured in Waterford, whence they were exported in great quantities. MORRYSON *Itin.* Part III. p. 100.

P. 54. Line 4. May under his mantle, go privily armed, &c.

This suspicion of Spencer, it is very probable, arose from his knowledge of a similar custom having prevailed on the continent, while the *Cappes*, answering to the Irish mantles, were in use. This custom is alluded to in the old tale of *Aucassin et Nicolette*.—" Tout-à-coup il apperçut venir du haut de la rue les soldats du guet qui faisaient leur ronde, armée *d'épées nues cachées sous leurs cappes.*"

P. 58. Line 4. Before we dispatch the reign of our virgin Queen, &c.

From the following anecdote in *The memoirs of Sir James Melville*, it appears, that perfumes, which might be found breathing from every box on the toilets of the English ladies in this reign, were now unknown in Ireland, or at least but partially used. Sir James having described his voyage to Ireland, and acquainted us with the tarrying the night of his arrival at the house of a son-in-law of Odocart, an Irish chieftain, situate on the border of a lake, proceeds to narrate that " the next morning Odocart came there, and
" convoyed us to his house, which was a great dark tower, where we had cold chear, as
" herring and biscuit ; for it was Lent. There finding two English gray friars who had
" fled out of England, the said friars perceiving the bishop to look very kindly to Odo-
" cart's daughter, who fled from him continually ; they brought to him a woman who
" spoke English, to ly with him. Which harlot being kept quietly in his chamber, found
" a little glass within a case standing in a window ; for the coffers were all wet with the
" sea-waves that fell into the ship, during the storm. She believing it had been ordained
" to be eaten, because it had an odoriferous smell, therefore she licked it clean out ;
" which put the bishop into such a rage, that he cried out for impatience, discovering his

" harlotry and his choler in fuch fort as the friars fled, and the woman followed. But
" the Irifhmen and his own fervants did laugh at the matter; for it was a vial of the moft
" precious balm that grew in Egypt, which Solyman the great Turk had given in a pre-
" fent to the faid bifhop, after he had been two years ambaffador for the King of France
" in Turky, and was efteemed worth 2000 crowns." Oct. ed. p. 16.

P. 58. Note *(d)*. The art of knitting, it is moft probable, was now unknown in Ireland, &c.

It fhould not be forgotten that the Dublin Society gave Michael Bane of Dublin a pre-mium of twenty five pounds, in the year 1742, for his invention of making ribbed ftockings, and twilling them withinfide.

P. 60. Line 20. We will now proceed to the reign of James I.

From a portrait of one of the St. Lawrence family painted in 1511, it appears, that Ruffs and Rings were worn by the higher claffes of the Irifh in this reign. This portrait is ftill preferved in the Caftle of Howth.

P. 62. Line 1. Their heads be covered after the Turkifh manner, with many elles of linen, &c.

This fafhion ftill prevails here. Col. Vallancey informs me, that he has feen the heads of feveral female peafants in Fingal, and in the interior parts of the kingdom, dreffed after this manner.

P. 62. Line 8. The very chiefs of the Irifh, as well men as women, goe naked in very winter time, &c.

In this affertion Morryfon certainly departs from truth, as I have already attempted to fhew. However it is faid that the Celtæ defpifed death fo much, as often to fight naked. It is alfo faid that the Highlanders, as if in obfervance of this barbarous cuftom, threw off their plaids and fhort coats, and fought in their fhirts, fo late as the battle of Killi-krankie.—

krankie.—CLAVIGERO in his valuable history of Mexico, informs us, that the common soldiers in that country went entirely naked except the maxtlati, or girdle; on which he very sensibly remarks that " the European historians, who express so much wonder " at this, have not observed how common the same practice was amongst the ancient " nations of Europe itself." Vol. 1. p. 367.

P. 69. Note *(b)*. For the manner in which the State officers, &c.

I shall here transcribe the passage to which I refer. " About the 18th of May 1613, the " lord deputy, with all the peers of the realm, and the clergy, both bishops and archbi- " shops, attired in *Scarlet robes* very sumptuously, with sound of trumpets; the lord " David Barry, viscount Buttevant, bearing the sword of State, and the earl of Tho- " mond, bearing the cap of maintenance; and after all these, the lord deputy followed, " riding upon a most stately horse, very richly trapped, himself attired in a very rich " and stately *robe of purple-velvet*, which the King's Majesty had sent him, having his " train borne up by eight gentlemen of worth."—Mention of the dress of the State-officers, naturally leads me to give some account of the repository of the Wardrobe appertaining to the State.

The State-wardrobe continues to be kept in a tower called the Wardrobe-Tower, which now affords an entrance to the Chapel of the Castle of Dublin, and was formerly united to Birmingham Tower by a curtain. Though the office of Wardrobe-keeper of the Castle of Dublin, was probably coeval with the Tower, I have not been able to trace it higher in the records of our public offices than the 1st. Geo. I.—It was then conferred on Edward Butler, gent. being at that time, says his Majesty in his patent, " in our dispose," an expression from which its earlier existence may be inferred. The nature of the office and the fee, are thus set forth, with great simplicity of language, in the patent which I have just quoted. " Whereas the office of keeping, cleaning, airing and dressing up " of the houses, rooms, buildings and edifices erected, and to be erected within our cas- " tle of Dublin in our said kingdom of Ireland, and the keeping, cleaning, and ayring " of the robes, hangings and cloaths of State-chairs, stools, and other utensils usually " kept, and remaining within our said castle; and likewise the office of keeping, at- " tending and setting of the Clock within our said castle, were heretofore erected upon " very necessary and useful occasions for the good of our service, and two several fees

" amounting in the whole to sixteen pence Irish by the day, granting for the executing
" of the said several offices (that is to say) eight pence Irish by the day for the keeping,
" cleaning, ayring and dressing up of the houses, rooms, buildings, and edifices erected
" and to be erected within our said castle of Dublin, and the keeping, cleaning and ayr-
" ing of the said robes, hangings and cloaths of State-chairs, stools, and other utensils
" usually kept, and remaining within our said castle; and the like sum of eight pence
" Irish by the day, for keeping, and setting of said clock; lodgings, likewise within the
" said castle for him that should execute the said office to reside in, &c." Aud. Gen. Off.

P. 70. Note *(f)*. The first person recorded to have worn a wig in England, &c.

It is said that the first person by whom a wig was worn in Ireland, was a Mr. Edmund O'Dwyer, who lost his estate by joining in the opposition to Cromwell's forces. He was known amongst the vulgar by the appellation of *Edmund of the Wig*.

P. 80. Line 2. From the accession of George I. to the present day, Fashion has been such a varying Goddess, &c.

Amongst many other ridiculous fashions that prevailed in this country, since the reign of queen Anne, was that of the ladies wearing bed-gowns in the streets, about forty years ago. The canaille of Dublin were so disgusted with this fashion, or perhaps deemed it so prejudicial to trade, that they tried every expedient to abolish it;—they insulted in the streets and public places those ladies who complied with it, and ridiculed it in ballads. But the only expedient that proved effectual was the prevailing on an unfortunate female who had been condemned for a murder, to appear at the place of execution in a bed-gown.

I shall conclude these notes with dean Swift's *Epilogue to a Play for the benefit of the weavers in Ireland*, performed at Dublin about the year 1721, in which are specified the several fabrics for Dress manufactured in Ireland, particularly in Dublin, in the reign of George I.

> Who dares affirm this is no pious age,
> When charity begins to tread the stage?
> When actors, who at best are hardly savers,
> Will give a night of benefit to weavers?

Stay,

Stay,—let me fee, how finely will it found !
Imprimis, from his Grace an hundred pound.
Peers, clergy, gentry, all are benefactors;
And then comes in the *Item* of the actors.
Item, the actors freely gave a day,——
The poet had no more, who made the play."
" But whence this wond'rous charity in play'rs?
They learnt it not at fermons, or at pray'rs:
Under the rofe, fince here are none but friends,
(To own the truth) we have fome private ends.
Since waiting-women, like exacting jades,
Hold up the prices of their old brocades;
We'll drefs in manufactures made at home,
Equip our Kings and Generals at the Comb (b):
We'll rig in Meath-ftreet Ægypt's haughty Queen;
And Anthony fhall court her in *Ratteen*.
In *blue Shalloon* fhall Hannibal be clad,
And Scipio trail an *Irifh purple Plad*.
In *Drugget* dreft, of thirteen pence a yard,
See Phillip's fon, amidft his Perfian guard;
And proud Roxana fir'd with jealous rage,
With fifty yards of *Crape*, fhall fweep the ftage.
In fhort, our Kings and Princeffes within,
Are all refolv'd the project to begin;
And you, our fubjects, when you here refort,
Muft imitate the fafhion of the Court."
" Oh ! cou'd I fee this audience clad in *Stuff*,
Tho' money's fcarce, we fhould have trade enough :
But chints, brocades, and lace, take all away,
And fcarce a crown is left to fee a play:
Perhaps you wonder whence this friendfhip fprings
Between the weavers and us play-houfe kings:
But wit and weaving had the fame beginning;
Pallas firft taught us poetry and fpinning :

And

(b) " A ftreet in Dublin famous for woollen manufactures."

94 ADDITIONAL NOTES.

And next obferve how this alliance fits,
For weavers now are juft as poor as wits:
Their brother quill-men, workers for the ftage,
For forry *Stuff* can get a crown a page;
But weavers will be kinder to the play'rs,
And fell for *twenty pence a yard* of theirs."
And, to your knowledge, there is often lefs in
The poet's wit, than in the player's dreffing."

WARD-ROBE TOWER of DUBLIN CASTLE.

MEMOIR

ON THE

ARMOUR and WEAPONS

OF THE

IRISH.

TO

The Right Honourable

E L I Z A B E T H

COUNTESS of MOIRA.

Madam,

Emulating the devotion of a Grecian Warrior, I determined to sacrifice to Minerva before I entered the field. Hence this address to your Ladyship. But the offering which I am now laying at your Ladyship's feet, is not made so much with a View of courting your protection, as to evince my gratitude. As such I flatter myself it will be received, and as such, I humbly hope, it will be acceptable.

If I have conferred any obligation on my Countrymen by giving them this Memoir, it is to you, MADAM, their thanks are due. When your LADYSHIP condescended to promote my enquiries concerning the National Dress of the Irish, the light which you shed on that subject, beamed occasionally on their Armour and Weapons. Struck with a few peculiarities in them, I was induced to a closer inspection. The result of this scrutiny was the little Memoir which now, like the wandering Stream, naturally returns

"Al mar, dov' ella nacque."

I have the honor to be,
MADAM,
Your LADYSHIP's
Much obliged,
Most humble, and
Most devoted Servant,

Joseph Cooper Walker.

MDCCLXXXVIII.

MEMOIR
ON THE
ARMOUR and WEAPONS
OF THE
IRISH.

A MORE extended and accurate account of the Armour and Weapons of the Irish than is commonly to be found, will not, it is hoped, be unacceptable to the Antiquarian Reader, nor be deemed an unnecessary appendage to the history of our national Dress. The few incidental notices of these subjects scattered in the foregoing Essay, may rather have excited than gratified curiosity: They certainly merit a more ample detail than either my abilities or materials can promise. Few are the remains of heroes or their Arms floating on the ocean of time.—

―――― " Pauci in gurgite vasto
Apparent nantes."

I do

I do not mean to pursue the enquiry on which I am now entering, into remote ages: the Armour and Weapons of the early Irish lie " hid in night," and I do not feel myself stimulated by the spirit of Quixotism to go in quest of them. The manner in which the Irish protected their bodies, and assailed their enemies in the field of battle, before the invasion of the Danes, history has indeed recorded; but in recording those circumstances, she too often committed her pen to the hand of fancy. Previous, then, to that event, her authority is questionable; and as such I wish to be understood as considering it, whenever I may be found appealing to it.

As the Irish usually adopted the Weapons and Armour of the different nations by whom they were severally invaded and harrassed, there can be but few national peculiarities in their Arms or Martial habiliments. I shall therefore endeavour to treat these subjects with as much brevity as may be consistent with perspicuity. The trouble of description (except in a few instances,) has been saved me by Pere Daniel and Mr. Grose: We shall find but few articles in the camp-wardrobe of the Irish warrior, that have not been minutely described by those learned gentlemen.

With a view to that brevity which I have promised to observe, I shall divide this Memoir into four heads, viz.—ARMOUR, WEAPONS, ARCHERY, and FIRE-ARMS. And under these heads I shall dilate severally and historically on the different articles which they involve.

ARMOUR.

ARMOUR.

(HELMET)

Cailmhion, Salet, Scull.

FROM some Coins of Irish reguli found at Ballylinam in the Queen's county, in the year 1786, it appears that the open Helmet was worn in Ireland so early as the tenth century, the period to which those Coins are assigned (a). But a more indubitable monument of the Armour which protected the head of the Irish in the next century, is presented us on the tomb of O'Conor, at Roscommon. Plate IV. The form of this Helmet differing from that of any other nation, I am inclined to think it was peculiar to Ireland, and that it is alluded to in Antiqitates Celto-Scandicæ, under the title of " Pileum Hibernicum (b)." This Cap or Helmet was first made of the skin of a beast, and then called Cailmhion: soon as iron was introduced, it was made of that metal. The flat helmet which prevailed in England in the time of Henry II. must have found its way into Ireland at a very

---

(a) *Trans. of the Royal Irish Acad.* 1787. See also Simon's *Essay on Irish Coins.* Plate I.

(b) P. 248.

early period; for we find it on an ancient monument at Old Kilcullen in the county of Kildare. Plate XII. fig. 2. But this helmet soon yielded its protection of the head to the Salet, which is preserved on a monument at Lusk, (in the county of Dublin,) of the fifteenth century. Plate XII. fig. 1.

While the Irish continued to trade with the Norwegians and Ostmen, it may be presumed that they adopted their mode of defending the head, as they did their arms, and manner of fighting *(c)*. But soon as the English had drawn the pale around their conquests, such of the inhabitants as were compelled to drag a miserable existence beyond that barrier, could no longer afford to cover their heads with metal, and were of course necessitated to rely on the resistance of their matted locks. At length this necessity became the fashion of their choice, and we find the body-guards of O'Neil appearing at the court of Elizabeth with uncovered heads, to the great amazement of the Londoners. This custom is noticed by Spencer, who gives it a Scythian origin. " Their " going to battle without armour on their bodies or heads, (says he) " but trusting to the thickness of their Glibs, the which, they say, will " sometimes bear off a good stroke, is meer Scythian *(d)*."

However, such of the Irish lords, knights and esquires as were under the subjection of the English, were obliged to provide the Yeomen in their service with Salets, by a Statute of Henry VII. intituled, An Act

(c) CAMBRENSIS.

(d) View of the State of Irel.—SPEED somewhere says, that the ancient Britons did not use casque or helmet.

ACT THAT THE SUBJECTS OF THIS REALME SHALL HAVE BOWES AND OTHER ARMOUR *(e)*. To the Galloglaſſes was given the iron Scull, the ſimpleſt of all helmets. This was alſo worn by Yeomen in the reign of Henry VIII. *(f)*. Several Sculls were extant in the armory of the Caſtle of Dublin not many years ſince, but not one remains in it at this day : two however are happily preſerved in the great hall of the caſtle of Howth, in the county of Dublin (*g*).

(e) As this act contains ſeveral curious particulars reſpecting the arms and armour of the Iriſh, I have given it at full length in No. IV. of the Appendix.

(f) HARRIS' *Hibern.* p. 92. Oct. ed.

(*g*) In the ſame caſtle is alſo preſerved a bar helmet, which was worn ſome ages ſince by one of the family of St. Lawrence.

Jack, Corselet, Haubergeon.

IT should seem that body-armour of any kind was unknown to the Irish previous to the tenth century, as we find King Murkertagh, in that century, obtaining the ascititious name of *Muirkertach na Geochall croceann* for so obvious an invention as that of the leathern Jacket. Yet coats of mail are mentioned in the BREHON LAWS, and the word Mail is supposed to be derived from *Mala* in Irish. Tho' the poets of the middle ages describe the heroes of Ossian as shining in polished steel, no relic of that kind of armour has escaped the wreck of time in Ireland; nor has there even a specimen of the brass armour in which the Danes so often met the Irish, fallen under my observation. Smith indeed tells us, that Corselets of pure gold were discovered on the lands of Clonties in the county of Kerry (*h*); but these might have been left there by the Spaniards who had a fortification called Fort del Ore, adjoining those lands.

That the bodies of the Irish should have been totally defenceless, with respect to armour, during their several bloody contests with the Danes, I am neither prepared to admit nor to deny; but confess myself inclined to think, that their inflexible attachment to their civil Dress would not yield to the fashion of the martial garb of their enemies, though it gave those people an evident advantage over them in the field of battle. It is certain that the English did not find them cased in

(*h*) *Nat. and Civ. Hist. of Kerry*, p. 187. One of these Corselets was purchased by Mr. O'HALLORAN, the gold of which was so ductile as to roll up like paper. *Introd. to Hist. of Irel.* p. 210.

AND WEAPONS OF THE IRISH. 107

in armour. In the moment of danger, Maurice de Prindergaft, one of the firſt Engliſh invaders, thus encouraged his followers: " We are well armed, and they (the Iriſh) are *naked (i)*." Nay even ſo late as the reign of Queen Elizabeth, Spencer repreſents the Iriſh as going to battle without armour *(k)*.

But the pains taken by the Engliſh to oblige ſuch of the Iriſh as were within reach of their iron graſp, to aſſimilate with themſelves in cuſtoms and manners, gradually ſpread the Engliſh modes within the Pale *(l)*. Accordingly we find an ancient monumental figure at Old Kilcullen in the county of Kildare, dreſſed in the chain mail *(m)* that prevailed in England about the reign of Henry II. Plate XII. fig. 2.

The authoritative voice of Parliament too was raiſed to recommend the military dreſs of the Engliſh. By the Statute of Henry VII. which I have juſt cited, the Iriſh nobility and gentry who wore the Engliſh yoke, were directed to provide their yeomen with Jacks as well as Salets. It may therefore be inferred that all the ſoldiers within the pale were clad in this kind of Armour.

The Jack of the Iriſh is depicted on O'Conor's tomb at Roſcommon. Plate IV. and is deſcribed by Spencer as being made of quilted leather, embroidered

---

(*i*) HARRIS' *Hibern.* p. 17.

(*k*) *View of the State of Irel.*

(*l*) That in latter days pains were taken to ſpread thoſe modes beyond the Pale, may be preſumed from the following article in the Charter granted to Galway in 1559.— " That the mayor from time to time do take the muſter and view of all the able men, and of their *furniture* and *armour.*"

(*m*) When the Iriſh clergy quarrelled amongſt themſelves, they ſometimes threw off
their

embroidered with gilded leather, like the robe of Shecklaton in which Chaucer habits his fir Thopas *(n)*.—

> His robe was of *Chekelatoun*
> That cofte many a jane *(o)*.

But the learned Mr. Tyrwhitt will not admit that the Irifh Jacket bore any refemblance to fir Thopas' robe, and affigns incontrovertible reafons for diffenting from the opinion of Spencer; however he does not attempt to difpute the fidelity of his defcription *(p)*. Inftead of gilded leather, the Jacket was fometimes embroidered with filk, of which an inftance is given in THE CHRONICLE OF IRELAND publifhed by Holinfhed *(q)*.

As

---

their gowns, and covered their caffocks with coats of mail. See an inftance under the year 1381, in *Mon. Hib.* p. 208.

(n) *View of the State of Irel.* p. 224. fol. ed.

(o) Cant. Tales by TYRWHITT, Vol. II. p. 231.

(p) Ibid. Vol. IV. p. 315. Since writing the above, a little reflection has leffened with me the force of Mr. Tyrwhitt's objection, which feems to arife principally from the prefumption, that the robe was worn by knights only in time of peace. Now Mr. Tyrwhitt's memory muft have failed him on this occafion, for he could not have been ignorant, that the knights often fought, at leaft in the lifts, in long robes that came down to their heels. *Mem. of Chival.* p. 234.

(q) P. 91.

AND WEAPONS OF THE IRISH.

As well as leathern, thrum Jackets were sometimes worn by the Irish. It was in this kind of Jacket, according to Camden, that O'Neal's attendants were clad. For a curious observation on the thrum jacket, I shall here take leave to refer the reader to page 57. of the foregoing Essay.

Although we are taught by Stanihurst and Spencer to believe, that the Jack or Jacket was uniformly the armour of the Galloglasses, yet we find that they sometimes wore the Haubergeon *(r)*, which, as well as the Jacket, was of English origin. This species of armour is thus minutely and satisfactorily described by the learned editor of Blount's ANTIENT TENURES. " The Haubergeon (says he) was a coat com-
" posed of several folds of coarse linen, or hempen cloth; in the midst
" of some of which was placed a sort of net-work, of small ringlets
" of iron, about a quarter of an inch diameter, interwoven very ar-
" tificially together, in this manner; and in others of thin iron square
" plates, about an inch from side to side, with a hole in the midst of
" each, the edges laid one over another, quilted through the cloth
" with small pack thread, and bedded in paper covered with wool *(s)*.

The religious military orders also contributed to introduce the use of Armour. Sepulchral figures in the habits of Knights' Templars remain in different parts of this kingdom. The 13th baron of Howth reposes beside his wife in that dress. In the Cathedral of Kildare, we find one of the Fitz-Gerald family similarly habited. And in Plate XII. fig. 1. is represented the figure of a knight templar, from a
sketch

(r) HOLINSHED *Conq. of Irel.* p. 7.

(s) P. 92.

sketch made by my brother, under my own eye, in the year 1784, from a tomb at Lusk in the county of Dublin.

(SHIELD.)

Target, Pavice.

ON this subject I cannot promise much satisfaction. That the Shields of the early Irish were not made of metal may be safely inferred from the circumstance of there being but a single instance of a metal shield having been found in our bogs, so replete with almost every other implement of war. Their form, however, is determined by Spencer, who tells us, that they were long and broad; and adds that they were made of wicker rods (*t*). Hence we may conclude that the Irish shield resembled the Roman Scutum, and like it too, was sometimes large enough to convey the killed or wounded from the field of battle. In the poem of THE DEATH OF OSCAR, the grandson of the celebrated Fin Mac Cumhal, the author thus pathetically describes the manner in which the wounded hero was borne from the plains of Gabhra.—" We *lifted the noble Oscar high upon our Shields*,
" and carried him away with care, until we came to the house of Fin.
" The howling of the dogs by our side, the groans of the aged chiefs,
" the lamentations of all the Fians. It was this that afflicted my
" heart

(*t*) *View of the State of Irel.*

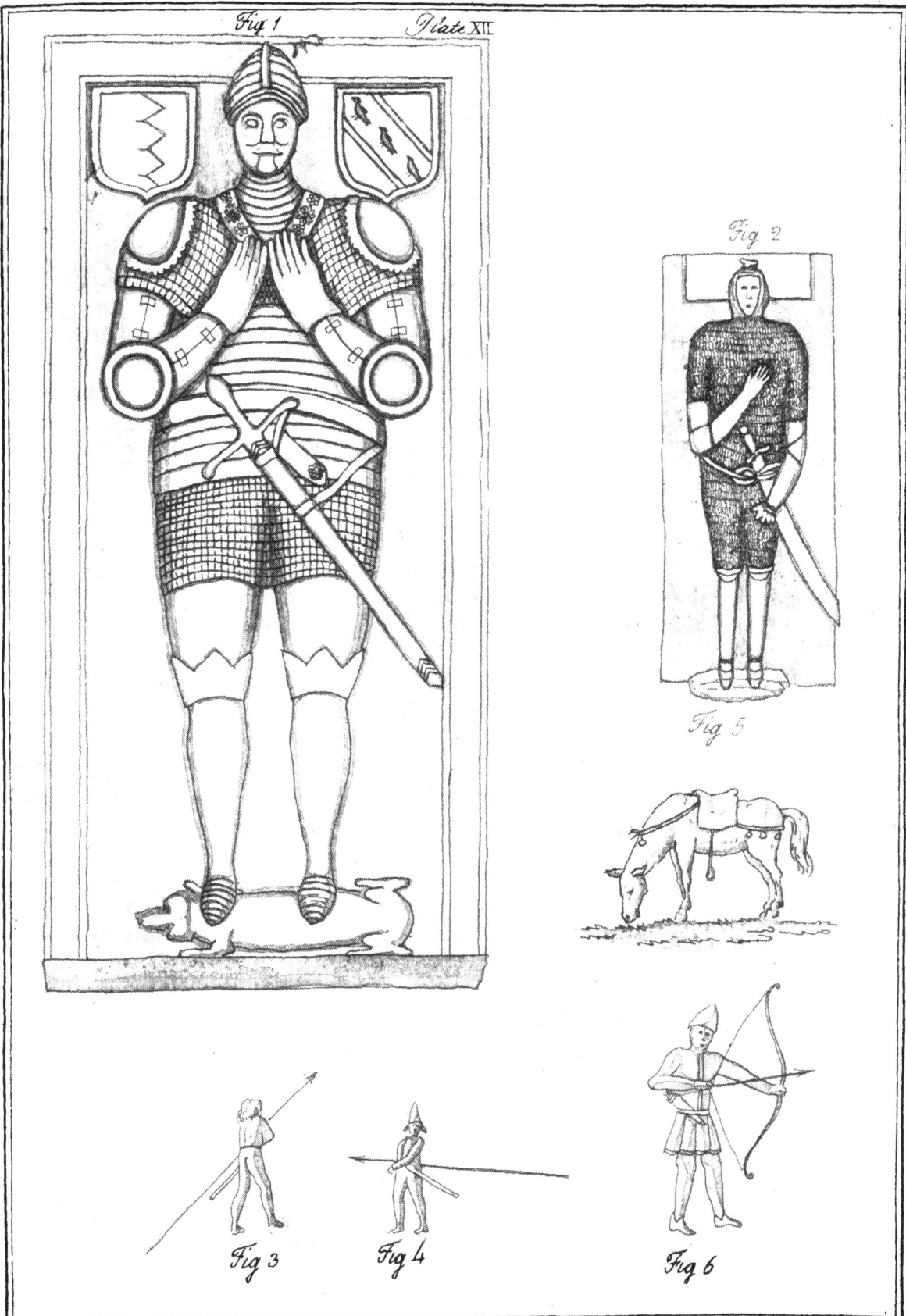

AND WEAPONS OF THE IRISH.

" heart. No mother lamented her son, nor one brother for another,
" but each of us that was present wept for Oscar (*u*)."

In another place Spencer tells us, that in many parts of Ireland,
" round leather Targets (*w*) coloured after the Spanish fashion" were

in

(*u*) *Transf. of the Royal Irish Acad.* Antiq.

(*w*) In the memorable single combat between the O'Conor's before the lords justices within the walls of the Castle of Dublin, A. D. 1583, we find the parties armed with *Targets*. Having mentioned this combat, I shall transcribe Mr. HARRIS' detail of it, as it will serve to acquaint the reader with the manner in which tournaments were sometimes conducted in Ireland. " The challenge being accepted by the appellant, all things
" were prepared to try the issue, and time and place appointed, according to precedents
" drawn from the laws of England in such cases. The weapons, being Sword and
" *Target*, were chosen by the defendant, and the next day appointed for the combat.
" The lords justices, the judges, and counsellors attended in places set apart for them,
" every man according to his rank, and most of the military officers for the greater so-
" lemnity of the trial, were present. The combatants were seated on two stools, one
" at each end of the inner court of the Castle. The court being called, the appellant
" was led forward from his stool within the lists, stripped to his shirt, and searched by
" the Secretary of State, having no arms but his sword and *Target*; and taking a corporal
" oath, that his quarrel was just, he made his reverence to the lords justices and the court,
" and then was conducted back to his stool. The same ceremony was observed as to
" the defendant. Then the pleadings were openly read, and the appellant was demand-
" ed, whether he would aver his appeal? Which he answering in the affirmative, the de-
" fendant was also asked, whether he would confess the action, or abide the trial of the
" same? He also answered, that he would aver his plea by the sword. The signal being
" given by the sound of trumpet, they began the combat with great resolution. The
" appellant received two wounds in his leg, and one in his eye, and thereupon attempted
" to close the defendant, who being too strong for him, he pummeled him, till he
" loosened his murrion, and then with his own sword cut off his head, and on the point
" thereof presented it to the lords justices, and so his acquittal was recorded." *Hist. of Dublin.* pag. 50, 51.

in ufe. However willing I may be to fubfcribe to Spencer's opinion on any occafion, I cannot entirely agree with him on this point. It was certainly from the Danes, not from the Spaniards, that this fafhion of the fhield was borrowed by the Irifh (*x*). One of the writers who contributed to Holinfhed's CHRONICLE, thus defcribes the army led by Hafculphus againft Dublin, in the reign of Henry II.—" They " were all mightie men of warre, and well appointed after the Danifh " maner, being harneffed with good brigandines, jacks, and fhirts of " male ; their *fhields*, *bucklers*, and *targets were round*, and *coloured red*, " and *bound about with iron*." The Irifh might alfo have been confirmed in this fafhion of the fhield by the Englifh, amongft whom it prevailed anterior to the days of Spencer. See THE PROCESSION OF KING EDWARD VI. a very curious engraving lately publifhed by the fociety of Antiquaries of London.

According to the BREVIATE of Baron Finglas, the Pavice was in ufe in Ireland during the reign of Henry VIII.—" Item, That no Englifh- " men dwellinge within Maghregron doe take no fpear with him to the " field, except he haith a Bowe or *Pavice* (*y*), upon paine of forfeiting " fix

---

(*x*) A friend cenfured this conclufion as being rather rafh, and adduced MOUNTFAUCON to prove, that the fafhion of the ancient Spanifh Shield and that of the Irifh in the time of Spencer, were very fimilar. *Antiq.* Vol. VII. chap. I. book 3. Without enquiring here whence the Irifh derived the round Shield, I fhall obferve, that it muft certainly have obtained at very remote periods amongft them, as the Shield is often compared by the old Irifh poets to the full moon, in allufion, no doubt, to its rotundity.

(*y*) See the Pavice or Pavais defcribed by GROSE, p. 27. and GUILLIM, p. 5.

" six shillings and eight pence, and losing of his Spear, toties quo-
" ties."

We are told by Mr. Macpherson, that the early Irish and Scots summoned their tribes together by means of the sound of a Shield suspended to a tree and struck with the butt end of a spear (*q*). On such an occasion, it is natural to suppose, that a brass or metal shield of some kind must have been used: yet no metal shield (save one) as I have already observed, has been found in this kingdom; nor can I learn that the Scots boast of having discovered any (*r*). It has indeed been asserted, that silver Shields were formerly, not only used but forged in Ireland. But as this assertion has neither been supported by contemporary writers, nor by a specimen, we are at liberty to question it. It is, however, a well attested fact, that a golden Shield, or rather a Shield adorned with gold, was found not many years since near Lismore in the county of Corke, by three peasants who sold it for seventy guineas to a neighbouring silver smith. By this relation I do not mean to insinuate, that golden Shields were borne in common by the Irish, though it may afford good grounds for a presumption, that they were sometimes carried before the leaders of their armies, flashing terror, like the Ægis of Minerva: nor do I mean to insinuate that this Shield was manufactured here; I am rather inclined to think that it was left by some of the Northern invaders, amongst whom golden Shields were prevalent. Unwilling to advance any position without proof, I shall take occasion to cite in
this

(*q*) Ossians *Poems*, Vol. II. p. 84. There is at this day a proverbial expression amongst the vulgar Irish, that implies *striking the wicker*, by which a challenge is understood; so that Mr. Macpherson's assertion is not without foundation.

(*r*) According to Guillim, (*Disp. of Heraldry*) the Highlanders' Shields were made of wicker, and covered with skins.

this place, a paffage from a tranflation of a curious inedited Icelandic manufcript of the tenth century intituled, A Voyage to Ireland undertaken from Iceland (s), in which Olave, the hero, is introduced in the martial habiliments of Iceland, bearing a golden Shield on his arm. The veffel which conveys Olave to Ireland in queft of his reputed father, the then reigning monarch, being ftranded on the Irifh coaft, the neighbouring inhabitants pour down in a body on the ftrand, in order to capture it. It is in the act of repulfing this lawlefs mob that Olave is introduced in the manner I have mentioned.—" The
" Irifh hearing this, prepared to attack the veffel with an univerfal fhout.
" For this purpofe they proceeded towards her with an intent to draw
" her on fhore, as the water was not deeper than their armpits, or the
" girdle of the talleft. The place, however, where the veffel rode, was
" deep enough to keep her afloat. At the inftance of Olave, his com-
" panions feized their arms and ranged them along the fides between
" the ftem and the ftern, which they covered with Shields, forming,
" as it were, a kind of breaft-work or parapet, the lower part of
" which was filled with fpears, for the purpofe of being in readinefs
" This being done, Olave afcended the prow, arrayed in a Gorget; his
" head invefted with a gilded helm, and a gold hilted fword by his fide;
" and in his hand he held a lance formed hook-wife, calculated as well
" for ftabbing as for cutting. The Shield with which he covered his
" breaft, was blazoned with a *lion of gold.*"

Before I difmifs this article I fhall obferve, that the lofs of a Shield was not lefs ignominious amongft the early Irifh, than formerly amongft the Lacedemonians, and latterly in thofe nations, where the fpirit of chivalry prevailed (t).

WEAPONS.

(s) This MS. is in the collection of lord Rawdon.

(t) Grose's *Treat. on Anc. Armour*, p. 26.

WEAPONS.

Sword, Skian, or Skeine.

THE antiquity of the Sword is so remote, that I cannot venture to determine the period in which it was first wielded by the Irish. Before they had to contend with foreign invaders cased in armour, it is probable they used wooden Swords. This we can only conjecture from similar weapons having been found in nations amongst whom civilization had made but short advances. That both brass and iron Swords were in early use in Ireland is evident from several of each kind having been found in different parts of the kingdom, bearing the marks of high antiquity (*u*). Plate XIII. fig. 5. (*w*). The form of the Sword worn by the Galloglasses in the eleventh century, appears on O'Conor's tomb at Roscommon, Plate IV. In the fresco paintings at Knockmoy, so often mentioned, we have a delineation of a broad sword, Plate III. fig. 3. The knights templars Sword is sculptured on several monuments of the middle ages, Plate XII. fig. 1.

(*u*) *Collect. de Reb. Hib.* Vol. 1. p. 478.

(*w*) The engraving to which I refer was made after the delineation of a Sword given in the *Phil. Surv. of the South of Irel.* which the author says, was as exact a drawing as he could make of a brass Sword found in a bog near Cullen (county Tipperary) which is twenty two inches in length, and weighs near two pounds. This Sword, he observes, is of the same metal and construction of the Sword-blades lately found upon the plains of Cannæ, p. 160.

One of thefe was found not many years fince, on a tiled floor near the fite of the old Priory of Kilmainham, Plate XIII. fig. 3. (*x*). A two handed Sword wielded with great fuccefs by a baron of Howth, now hangs in the hofpitable hall of the caftle of that ancient family, Plate XIII. fig. 1. Some two-edged Swords, found in the bog of Cullen in the county Tipperary, are thus defcribed by governor Pownal in his lift of antiques difcovered in that bog at different times.

" 1748. A brafs weapon, two feet feven inches long, which was two-edged from the hilt to the point. Thefe edges very much refembled the fin which proceeds out of both fides of an eel, from the navel to the top of the tail. It feemed to have been caft in that form and never whetted. It was one inch and three-fourths broad near the hilt, from which, for four inches, it was diminifhed to an inch and a quarter. From thence to the middle it encreafed an inch and an half, and from thence it grew narrower to the termination in an acute point. The blade was near half an inch thick; the part taken for the hilt was about five inches, near an inch broad in the middle, but lefs toward the blade and the pommel; in it were fix rivets, each of which was about three-fourths of an inch long, and on one of them hung a thin piece of gold, which weighed twelve pennyweight nine grains."

" 1751. Such another weapon as that found in 1748, on the rivets of which was a plate of gold which covered one fide; at the end of which

(*x*) This Sword, through the politenefs of the right honourable general Pitt, and the friendfhip of Thomas Goold, efq; was for a while in my poffeffion. An iron Sword of the fame form and fize of that of general Pitt, is now in the collection of Wm. Deane, efq; of Palace-row, Dublin. It was found together with an helmet and feveral human bones, in finking the foundation of Mr. Deane's houfe.

which was a thing like the pommel of a small sword, with three links of a chain hanging out of it: all the gold together weighed three ounces three pennyweight eleven grains."

" A weapon of the same form of that described in 1748, but that the metal of this was more refined. A goldsmith upon trial found there was gold in it. Close to the hilt on the thick part was engraved an oblong square, about one inch and an half long, inlaid with pewter and copper."

Soon as the spirit of chivalry passed from the continent into this island, the Sword became so dear to the Irish warrior, that he determined it should descend with him into the tomb. Hence so many Swords have been found in the graves of departed heroes. I shall give two instances.—In sinking for the foundation of an house not many years ago near Ormond-bridge, Dublin, a tomb-stone was found, with the figure of a cross-legged knight (*y*) sculptured upon it; beneath this stone lay a human skeleton, with an iron Sword extended at its side. And on opening a carne lately in the county of Cavan, an urn was discovered, containing a brass Sword broken into three parts, with ashes and human bones intermingled.

I cannot find that the Irish warriors, like the heroes of the Round-Table, distinguished their Swords by proper names (*z*); but it is certain that

they

(*y*) This is the first instance that has reached my knowledge of the monument of a Crusader having been found in this kingdom.

(*z*) Yet there is a passage in HARRIS' *Hist. of Dublin*, which serves, indeed, in some degree, to refute this assertion. " A. D. 1029, he (Sitric, king of Dublin) was suc-
" ceeding

they were equally folicitous in adorning them. Solinus relates, that the Irish form the handles of their Swords from the teeth of large sea-monsters, which they polish to a most beautiful whitenefs (a). Golden hilted Swords (b) have been found in great abundance in this kingdom. And we are told in the life of St. Bridget, that the King of Leinster prefented to Dubtachus, her father, a Sword ornamented with many coftly jewels, which the pious virgin purloined from Dubtachus, and fold for the charitable purpofe of relieving the neceffities of the poor.

The fuperstitious veneration in which the Sword was held by the ancient Irish, is noticed by Spencer. " When they go to battail (he re-" lates) they fay certain prayers or charms to their Swords, making a " crofs therewith upon the earth, and thrufting the points of their " blades into the ground, thinking thereby to have the better fuccefs " in fight. Alfo they ufe commonly to fwear by their Swords." To thefe cuftoms, Spencer gives a Scythian origin, forgetting, in the warmth of his zeal to prove the defcent of the Irish from the Scythians, that

the

" ceeded by his fon Aulaffe Mac-Sitric, who the year following was taken prifoner by
" Mathew or Mathgaun O'Riagan, and obliged to pay for his ranfom 200 cows, 80
" British horfes, 3 ounces of gold, and a certain Sword called *Charles' Sword*; per-
" haps the Sword of Charles Knute, fon to the King of Denmark, who fell valiantly
" fighting in the plains of Clontarf." P. 198. But this paffage feems rather to record a Danifh than an Irifh cuftom.

(a) I faw, not long fince, a Sword anfwering the defcription of Solinus, which was found in the county of Clare.

(b) The Annalift of Innisfallen defcribes Brian Boroimhe exhorting his foldiers before the battle of Clontarf, with a crucifix in his left, and a *gold-hilted Sword* in his right hand.

the former cuftom muft have originated amongft chriftians, and that the latter was derived from the Danes (c).

As well in Ireland as in England and on the Continent, the Dagger, which the Irifh denominated a Skian, (Plate XIII. fig. 6.) was the conftant companion of the Sword. So early as the memorable battle of Clontarf we find an Irifh prince wearing one of thefe weapons in his Girdle (d); and in the Icelandic manufcript already quoted, it is mentioned as an Irifh weapon. The ufe of this inftrument, both as an ornament and defenfive weapon, continued through feveral ages down to very late times. It appears fticking in the Girdles of the Irifh Kings who paid homage to Rich. II. In the reign of Elizabeth, it was forbid, by her charter to Kilkenny, to leave its fcabbard in the time of a quarrel:—" to draw a Sword or *Skein* in a quarrel, was punifhable by the fine of a half a mark."—The author of HESPERI-NESO-GRAPHIA, gives it to his hero, Gillo. And in the celebrated ballad of the PLEARACA NA RUARCACH, it is given to all O'Rourke's guefts.

>They rife from their feaft,
>   And hot are their brains,
>   A cubit at leaft
>   The length of their *Skeans*.

(c) Vide BARTHOLINE, *De Caufis contemp. mort. apud Dan.*

(d) *Collect. de Reb. Hib.* Vol. I. pag. 531.

(STAFF-WEAPONS.)

FIADHGHA or CRANNUIBH, SPEAR, DART.

IN the early ages, while the Irish lived on the precarious support of the chace, the Fiadhgha or Crannuibh, was the weapon with which they killed their prey. It is said to have been then a kind of Spear or Javelin about five feet long and pointed with flint or bone, Plate XIII. fig. 8. To that end which remained in the hand, was affixed a thong of leather, by means of which either the beast was retained, or the Spear recovered. But soon as commerce spread her sails in our ports, and the productions of the useful arts were diffused through the kingdom, this weapon varied its materials and its form, and was employed as well in flaying the rational as the irrational creation. The researches of my learned friend colonel Vallancey have brought to light several Spear-heads of different fashions and different materials, which were found in this kingdom. Of these he has given engravings in his COLLECT. DE REBUS HIBERNICIS. Vol. IV. Plate XI. to which I shall refer my reader. But I shall first indulge him with a delineation of a brass Spear-head of an elegant form, which was found, with five more, in the year 1774, very near the surface of the earth under a carne in the King's county, Plate, XIII. fig. 2. The original is now in the possession of Mr. John Brownrigg of Dublin, a gentleman who unites with excellent abilities in his profession of a surveyor, a laudable passion for Irish antiquities.

The

The dextrous manner in which the Irish used the Lance, is thus minutely described by Stanihurst: " Hastas bene ponderosas, circa " medium manibus prehendunt, non ad latera sua, infra brachium ap- " ponendo; sed supra capita lacertis viribusque librando." " They " grasp about the middle heavy Spears, which they do not hold pen- " dant at their sides under their arms, but hurl with all their strength, " over their heads." This mode of exercise, according to Spencer, was borrowed from the English.? It is, however, alluded to in one of the poems which Macpherson attributes to Ossian. " Oscar hurled another Spear on high (as we thought high enough); so great was the force with which it was cast, that it struck Art to the ground as he was aiming his Spear at Oscar (*e*)."

Yet the Spear thus dexterously hurled by the Irish " swift as the dra- gon's flight" was of a very incommodious length. This appears as well from A MAP OF THE TAKING OF THE EARL OF ORMOND amongst the MSS. of Trinity-College, Dublin, (Plate XII. fig. 3. 4.) as from the following lines in Harington's translation of THE OR- LANDO FURIOSO. Speaking of the Irish, from his own observa- tion without any regard to his author, he says,

" Short Swords they use to carry and *long Darts*, To fight both neare and farre aloofe withall(*f*)."

And King Mc. Murrough is described by a follower of Richard II. as bearing a long Dart in his hand, which he cast from him with much

dexterity

(*e*) *Death of Oscar. Transf. of the Royal Irish Acad.* In the same poem I was sorry to find a poisoned Spear in the hand of an Irish hero. Perhaps this custom was borrowed from the Danes. They were certainly not always incapable of such baseness. Leartes fights Hamlet with a poisoned Sword.

(*f*) Book 10. St. 73. By " long Dart" in this passage, the Spear or Lance is meant.

dexterity *(g)*. By the same writer we are told, that the Irish cast their Darts with such might, as no Haubergeon or coat of mail were sufficient proof to resist their force, their Darts piercing them through both sides *(h)*. Cambrensis in his account of the weapons of the Irish in his time, mentions a short lance, but does not enable me to describe it. He also mentions Darts with the same laconism. These we know, were carried by the Kerns or Daltini:—but that is all we are told concerning them,—except that thongs of leather were sometimes fastened to them *(i)*.

But, it is in describing the

TUAGH

(g) HARRIS' *Hib.* p. 53.

(h) Ibid. p. 52.

(i) WARES' *Works*, Vol. II. p. 161. It is observed (I think by CAMPION) that as the Kern threw his dart he exclaimed faro! faro!—Thus the ancient knight called on the name of his mistress while advancing to the charge.—Besides throwing the dart, the Kerns were employed in flinging stones, which they performed with so much strength and ability, that you would think, says STANIHURST, they drove them, like a circle, in an perpetual gyration. I shall here take occasion to observe, that the Kerns were the third military order of the Irish, and that they are noticed thus by SHAKESPEAR in Hen. VI. Part II. Act 3. Sc. 5. when speaking of John Cade's military atchievements in Ireland—

> Full often, like a *shag-hair'd crafty Kern*,
> Hath he conversed with the enemy;
> And undiscover'd come to me again,
> And giv'n me notice of their villanies.

Tuagh Catha, or Battle-Axe,

THAT Cambrensis speaks with feeling and minuteness. These are his words literally translated.—" The Irish use three kinds of "arms, short lances and two darts, as also broad axes, excellently "well steeled, the use of which they borrowed from the Norwegians "and Ostmen. They make use of but one hand to the Axe when "they strike, and extend their thumb along the handle to guide the "blow, from which neither the crested helmet can defend the head, "nor the iron folds of the armour, the body; whence it has happened "in our time, that the whole thigh of a soldier, though cased in well "tempered armour, hath been lopped off by a single blow of the Axe, "the whole limb falling on one side of the horse, and the expiring body "on the other."

This weapon soon superceded the use of the Claidhamh or heavy iron Sword. As the Irish had three names for the Battle-axe, colonel Vallancey is at a loss to know, whether to consider them as distinguishing different weapons, or as several names for the same. He gives an engraving of one in fig. 11. Plate XI. of Vol. IV. COLLECT. DE REB. HIB. which he deems an excellent weapon for the defence of an entrenchment. From the large rivets he concludes it must have been mounted on a very strong shaft *(j)*. In Plate XIII. fig. 4. is delineated

---

(j) Collect de Reb. Hib. Vol. IV. p. 62. (No. 13.) Plate XI. fig. 11.—Mr. O'HAL-LORAN relates, that " gold of a particular colour and hardness, made for the purpose of lodging the poll axes of our antient mare-sloign, or cavalry, has been frequently found." *Introd. to Hist. of Irel.* p. 210.

neated an iron Axe calculated as well to ſtab as cut, but the ſpike being broken off, it is rendered imperfect. It was found in a grave in Lecale, county of Down, and is now in the collection of the Counteſs of Moira, to whom I am indebted for the drawing.

Truly ſenſible of the deſtructive powers of the Battle-axe, the Engliſh put it into the hands of the Galloglaſſes *(k)*. Plate IV. Plate XIII. fig. 7. Soon as this body of men, the bulwark of the Engliſh government in Ireland, was diſſolved, their weapons were transferred to

(*k*) The ſecond order of the military was that of the Galloglaſſes, a name, ſays Spencer, which doth diſcover them to be ancient Engliſh. The order is thus particularly deſcribed by Stanihurſt.—" Proximus eſt equitibus ordo pedeſtris, qui conſtat ex " quodam genere ſagatorum militum, quos iſti Galeglaſia appellant. Homines ſunt mag- " næ ſtaturæ, præter communem morem Corporati, fortes buſtuarii, ſanguinarii toti, " ac minime propitii milites. Humanum apud illos nihil tam eſt, quam odium huma- " nitatis. Habent tela pedalia, ſecuribus ſimilia et gemina, cultris tonſoriis pæne acutiora, " longiuſculis haſtilibus adfixa, quibus plagam gravem faciunt, ubi feriunt. Prius vero " quam aliquis in eorum collegium co-optatur, magna religione jurat, quoties in aciem " dimicationemque venit, nunquam tergiverſari : tametſi iſte mos antiquari incipiat. In " omni acri ac acerbi prælio, ſi ad manus veniatur, aut cito illi pereunt, aut cito peri- " munt.." *De Reb. Hib.* p. 41, 42. " The next order to the equeſtrian is the pedeſ- " trian (or foot), conſiſting of a certain claſs of cloaked ſoldiers, called Galloglaſſes. " They are men of huge ſtature, able-bodied beyond the generality of men, brave " ſwordſmen, but blood-thirſty, and ſtrangers to mercy. They bear weapons of a foot " in dimenſions, not unlike hatchets, double, and ſharp as the keeneſt knife : theſe " they affix to halberts ſomewhat longer, and with theſe they wound deſperately thoſe " whom they ſtrike. (Plate XIII. fig. 4.) Before any one is admitted into this order, " he is obliged to ſwear a ſolemn oath, that he will never turn his back on his enemy in " the field of battle, although time ſhould have ſlackened the rigour of this uſage ; he " muſt ſwear alſo, that if in any fierce and ſharp conteſt, he ſhould come to cloſe con- " flict, to the Halberdeers, an harmlefs guard that attends on the chief governor, and is now denominated the Battle-axe-guard *(l)*. As the Axe which is borne by this guard varies in form from the ancient Tuagh-Catha, I have given a delineation of it in Plate XIII. fig. 10.

The dexterity with which it appears, the Irifh ufed this Battle-axe evinces their fondnefs for it. It was probably in order that they might deal the more deadly ftrokes with this weapon, that, as Campion relates, they left the right arm of their children unchriftened *(m)*.

(SLINGS.)

Clochadh, Krann-Tabhall, Celt.

SLINGS are alfo numbered with the weapons of the Irifh. They were called Clóchadh, and Krann-Tabhall. The dexterity of the Irifh in the ufe of this weapon is likewife celebrated by Cambrenfis:

" They

"flict, he fhould either be killed himfelf or kill his adverfary."—While the cuftom of Livery prevailed, the Galloglafs was allowed one penny a day in lieu of livery. Finglass' *Brev*. And befides his ordinary, he was entitled to a mether of milk, as a privilege. *Lett. concerning the coaft of Antrim.* In an eftablifhment of James I. extant in the Audit. Gen. Office, I find the following article.—" Walter M$_c$Edmond, captain of Galloglaffes, at 12d. per diem, to ceafe upon death."

(l) Though this is a very ancient guard, I have not been able to trace it higher amongft the records in the Auditor Gen. Office, than the reign of Charles II. It then confifted of a captain at £11. 4s. per month—a lieutenant at £9. 16s.—two ferjeants at £2. 10s. —Sixty halberdeers at £2. 2s.—each, per month.

(m) P. 15. There is an hill in the county of Galway called Knocktuagha (the hill of

axes)

" they are alfo very dexterous and ready, (fays he) beyond all other
" nations, in flinging ftones in battle, when other weapons fail them,
" to the great detriment of their enemies (*n*). Here again this writer's feelings feem to be awake.

Mr. Harris not being able to difcover any defcription of the Krann-Tabhall, or wooden Sling, has recourfe to conjecture. " This fort
" of Sling, (fays he) from the material it was made of, feems to me
" to refemble that defcribed by Vegetius, as a ftaff four feet long, to
" which was faftened a Sling of leather, which driven forward by both
" hands directs a ftone almoft like a wild afs (*o*)."

I fhall here take occafion to obferve, that Mr. Owens, the editor of Rowland's MONA ANTIQUA, feems decidedly of opinion, that the Celt, an inftrument fo called from our ignorance of its ufe, was employed as a Sling-hatchet (*p*). I will here confefs myfelf neither prepared to fubfcribe to, nor to diffent from Mr. Owens' opinion; and proceed to

axes) from the circumftance of the Irifh having gained a victory over the Englifh there by means of their battle-axes.

(*n*) In a defcription of a battle in *The annals of Innisfallen*, it is related, that the ftones came in fuch rapid fhowers that they blunted the arrows in their flight. And in the fame work, ftones flung from the fling are compared to burfting clouds fhowering over the heads, helmets, arms and caps of the combatants..—In clearing away the ruins of an old caftle fome years fince, a friend of mine found feveral artificial heaps of ftones formed of black marble, and weighing about 7lb. each, which he concluded, were prepared for the ufe of the flingers appointed to the defence of the caftle.

(*o*) WARE's *Works*, Vol. II. p. 162.

(*p*) P. 86. Mr. Whitaker treats of the Celt with his ufual ingenuity and vivacity, and concludes with calling it a Britifh Mohawk. *Hift. of Manch.* v. 1. p. 18. oct. ed.

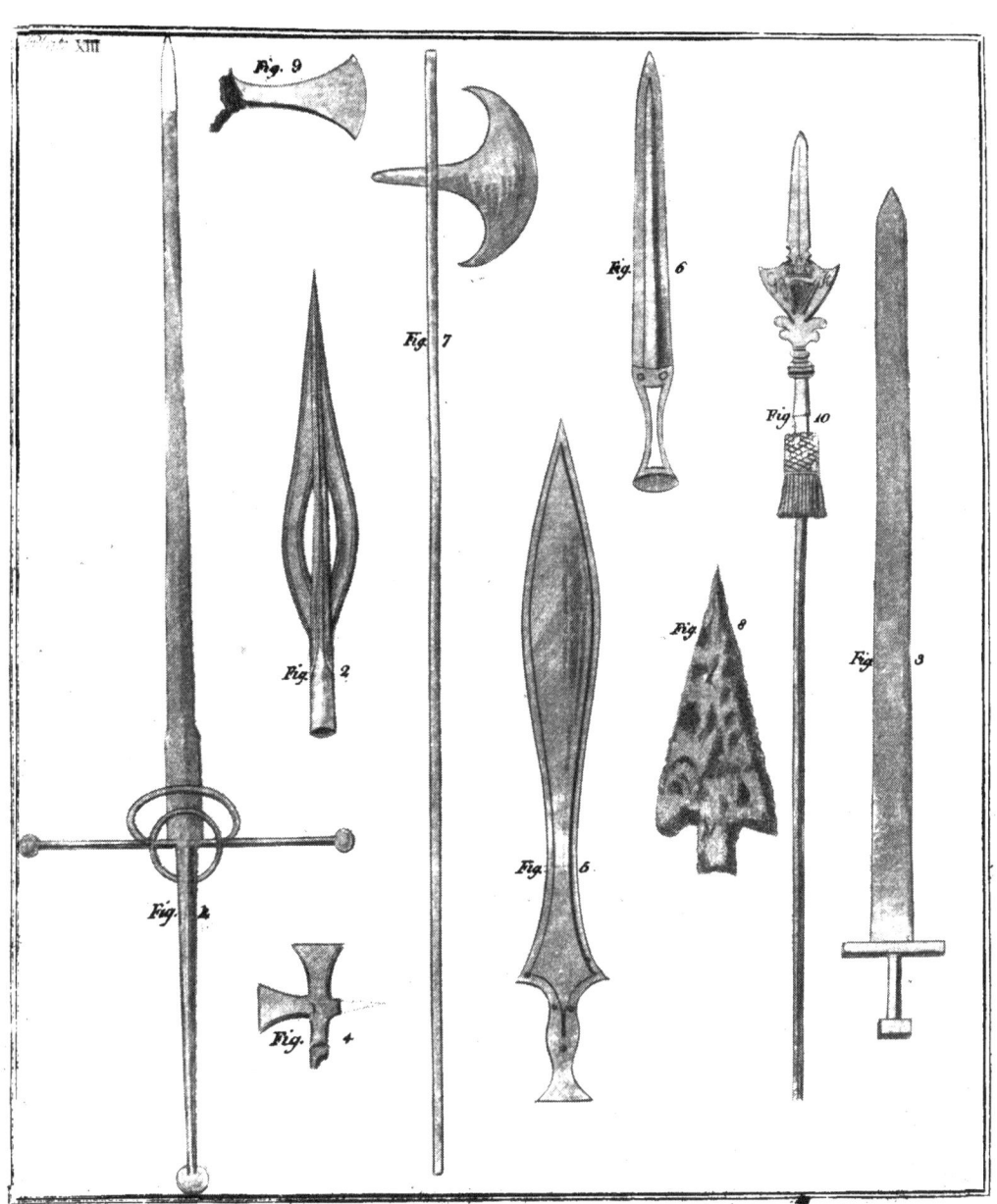

to close this article with relating, that great abundance of Celts have been found in this kingdom, together with several of the moulds in which they were cast (*q*). The

C r a n n i b h or C l u b

IS so obvious a weapon that it cannot be said to be peculiar to any nation or even to require a description; I shall therefore only observe, that in Ireland it was called Crannibh (*r*).

Having thus returned, as it were, to the Staff-weapons, I shall transcribe a passage relating to that article from Mr. O'Conor's DISSERTATIONS ON THE HISTORY OF IRELAND. "In process of time, (says "he) the Scots, through their intercourses with Gaul and Britain, made "some improvements in the fashion of their weapons. Thus, after "his return from his exile in Gaul, Labra-Loing seach, brought the "LAGEAN in use, a sort of broad-edged lance, from which the provin-"cialists of Leinster derived the name of Laighnidh, and their country "the name of Laghean (*s*)". This weapon, it may be presumed, soon fell into disuse, as we do not find it noticed by any of those writers who relate the wars of the Irish with the Danes, and the English.

ARCHERY.

(*q*) I remember to have seen a Celt with its mould produced (in the year 1788) in the committee of Antiquities of the Royal Irish Academy.

(*r*) In an insurrection in the friary of St. Saviour (county Dublin) in 1381, some of the brethren were armed with Clubs. *Mon. Hib.* p. 208.

(*s*) P. 85.

ARCHERY.

PERHAPS Archery can boaſt as high an antiquity in Ireland, as in almoſt any other nation of the earth. This will not be denied, if our obligations to the eaſt ſhould be admitted; for we find mention of Bows and arrows in Holy writ. Our old Chroniclers number Archery with the exerciſes of the militia commanded by the immortal Fin Mac Cumhal. And in other periods of Iriſh hiſtory, equally dark, we can ſometimes diſcern paſſing arrows piercing the gloom. Indeed, Spencer ſeems to inſinuate the early uſe of bows and arrows in Ireland: "Alſo their ſhort bows and little quivers, with ſhort bearded arrows, are very Scythian (*t*)." This ſhort bow was certainly not borrowed from the Engliſh, amongſt whom the croſs and long bow only were in uſe. Yet we have good reaſon to think, that Archery was totally difuſed in Ireland at the time of the Engliſh invaſion; for Cambrenſis repreſents the Iriſh as being ſo much annoyed by the arrows of the Engliſh, that we are led to infer they were a kind of offenſive weapons with which the Iriſh were then totally unacquainted. Another writer of the ſame period deſcribes the Iriſh avoiding the Engliſh forces "for fear of their archers (*u*)." Beſides, the feats of Archery performed by Robin Hood and his followers (who fled to Ireland in the reign of Richard I.) would not have been matter of ſo much aſtoniſhment to

the

(*t*) *View of the State of Irel.*

(*u*) HARRIS' *Hib.* p. 51.

the good people of Dublin, as we are told it was, had they been skilled in, or even acquainted with the practice (v).

But the English had not been long settled in Ireland when they imposed the practice of Archery on all the inhabitants of the Pale between sixty and sixteen years of age, by an act originating in their fears. This act was ordained in a Parliament holden at Trim in 5th Edward IV. and runs thus,—" Item, at the request of the commons,
" that consideration had to the great number of Irishmen, that exceed
" greatly the English people, that in force and augmentation of the
" King's lieges, it is ordeyned by authority of the said Parliament,
" That every Englishman and Irishman, that dwell with Englishmen
" and speak English, that betwixt sixty and sixteeen in age, shall have
" an English bow of his own length (w), and one fiftmele at the least
" betwixt

(v) Dr. HANMER tells us with great *naïveté*, that Little John (who followed his master to this country) " is said to have shot an Arrow a mile, and a great deal more," *Chron.* p. 179. In this relation the doctor not only evinces his credulity, but displays his ignorance of archery; for the ingenious and learned Mr. BARRINGTON, than whom no man can be better informed on the subject, thinks that eleven score and seven yards is the utmost extent that an arrow can be shot from a long bow. *Archæologia*, Vol. VII.—According to tradition, Little John shot an arrow from the Old-Bridge, Dublin, to the present site of St. Michael's church, a distance not exceeding, I believe, that mentioned by Mr. Barrington. But poor Little John's great practical skill in archery could not save him from an ignominious fate: it appeared from some records in the Southwell family, that he was publickly executed for robbery on Arbor-hill, Dublin.

(w) Mr. BARRINGTON considers this as a wise regulation.—" The regulation of the Irish Statute of Edward IV. viz. that the bow shall not exceed the height of the man, is allowed by archers to have been well considered; and as the arrow should be half the length of the bow, this would give an arrow of a yard in length to those only who were six feet high." Ibid.

" betwixt the necks, with twelve shafts of the length of three quarters
" of the standard, the bowes of ewe, wych-hassel, ashe, awburne, or
" any other reasonable tree acording their power, and the shafts in the
" same maner, within two moneths next after the publication of this
" estatute, on pain of two pence a man from moneth to other, till he
" shall have and continue the bow and shafts, and in lue of the bow
" and shafts broken and lost to have new, under pain of two pence
" every month till it be done. And yet not prohibiting gentlemen on
" horseback to ride according their best disposition to ride with
" spear, so that they have bowes with their men for time of necessitie."
And in the same Parliament there was ordained another ACT FOR HAVING A CONSTABLE IN EVERY TOWN, AND A PAIR OF BUTTS FOR SHOOTING, AND THAT EVERY MAN BETWEEN SIXTY AND SIXTEEN SHALL SHOOT EVERY HOLYDAY AT THE SAME BUTTS. The pain for offending against this act, was " one halfpenny for every day;" and the time of observance, " betwixt the first day of March and the last day of July."—In Plate XII. fig. 6. I have given the delineation of an Archer from an ancient painting.

In order the better to carry those acts into execution, by furnishing those whom they bound with a constant supply of bows, another act was passed in the eighth year of the same reign, to oblige " every mer-
" chant and passenger, that bring merchandises into this land of Ire-
" land out of England to the sum of an hundred pound, that he shall
" buy and bring with him into the said land in bows to the value of
" an hundred shillings, and so following after the rate under or over
" to the sum of twenty pounds."

But

But succeeding Kings either slackening the rigour of this act, or dispensing with the observance of it, the inhabitants of the Pale began to lack both bows and arrows. Of this remissness, it is probable, some of the Irish who had scorned the English yoke, took advantage, and others, according to an old English writer, "thereupon tooke hart "of grace, and practised our manners in shooting and the use of our "weapons; and by little and little they became so well expert and "skilfull therein, that whereas at the first they were easie to be over- "comed, were now strong and hardie, and not onlie able to resist, but "also readie to put us in danger and hazard (x)." To remedy these growing evils, an act was ordained in the 10th Henry VII. THAT THE SUBJECTS OF THIS REALME SHALL HAVE BOWES AND OTHER ARMOUR, LIKE AS THEY HAVE HAD IN TIMES PASSED.

In the next reign baron Finglass recommends, in his BREVIATE, "that shooting be used in every parish within the English pale every "holyday, so that the weather be fair, upon pain of three shillings and "four pence."

After this period we meet frequent mention of Archers attending the magistrates of the principal towns on martial and other expeditions; and a grant of poundage to the lord deputy to provide him with a guard of bowmen (y). But according as the use of fire-arms advanced, Archery lost ground, till at length it sunk into oblivion.

(x) *The Conq. of Ireland* in HOLINSHEDS' *Chron.* p. 52.

(y) FINGLASS, HARRIS.

The citizens of Dublin had their butts for many years on a plain in the village of Hogges, called Hoggin's-butt (now College-green), near a range of small houses denominated Tib and Tom. When the city spread over this green, the Butts were removed to that part of the North-strand, formerly called Cuningham's rope-walk, where my father remembers to have seen them, in the year 1734. About this time the practise of Archery totally ceased in Dublin, where it had been supported in its decline, by a society of gentlemen and eminent citizens, who called themselves The Archers' Club (z). The last member of this club was Mr. Henry Delamain, who lived and retained all his faculties to the year 1781. With this venerable Archer I shall close this article, and proceed to say a few words on the

Military Engines and Chariots

OF the Irish; whence I shall pass to their Fire-arms, with which article I shall conclude this Memoir.

CRAN-

(z) A sheaf of arrows which belonged to this club, is now in my possession. According to the tradition that was handed down with those arrows, they came from Nottingham. They are made of asp wood; feathered with a grey goose wing, and about twenty seven inches long. I have deposited one of them in the Museum of The Royal Irish Academy.

Cran-Tabhaill, Sow, Carab.

Mr. O'Connor tells us, " that in the reign of Crimthan ma Naire, " namely, in the firſt century, they (the Iriſh) got the uſe of the Cran- " Tabhaill, a machine from whence they ſhot ſtones on the enemy's en- " trenchments, or occaſionally on their ranks, in the day of battle *(a)*." But we hear no more of this engine, ſo may conclude its exiſtence was ſhort. The next engine that obtrudes its monſtrous bulk on our notice, is the Sow, which we find placed againſt the walls of Liſchane, in the year 1599. This engine, according to doctor Smith, was a kind of wooden houſe, that moved upon wheels, with doors opening inwards. It ſerved, he ſays, to cover the workmen who laboured with crows and pick-axes to make a breach.

Mr. O'Conor ſeems to ſpeak of the uſe of the Carab or military Chariot amongſt the early Iriſh, as an undoubted fact, and ſays that great feats are recorded of ſome of our ancient charioteers. And Mr. Harris obſerves, that in the TAIN-BO-CUAILGNE, military chariots and the manner of fighting in them, are deſcribed much after the way that Cæſar deſcribes the Britons fighting in the ſame ſort of carriage; and the guider of the chariot is there called Ara, a page or lacquey *(b)*.

Every

(a) Diſſ. on Hiſt. of Irel. p. 85.
(b) WARES' *Works,* Vol. II. p. 164.

Every reader of Ossian's poems must remember the beautiful description of the chariot of Cucholinn, the famous Irish chieftain, in the first book of FINGAL. But the blaze of splendour which Mr. Macpherson has thrown around this chariot, will not allow the eye to look steadily on it. In an Irish romance now lying before me of which the subject is the death of the same hero, his chariot is mentioned but not described: " Cucholinn having put on his helmet and habiliments of war, " leaped into his *Chariot* without taking leave of Cauff or his guests, " and his weapons fell down at his feet."

The chariot falling into disuse, the Irish were taught by the English to caparison the horses of their Cavalry with the strong brass bitt (*c*), sliding reins and shank pillion; (Plate XII. fig. 5.) and as well to mount without the aid of the stirrup, as to ride after the English fashion.

FIRE-

(*c*) Several bitts and spurs of fine workmanship have been found in our bogs and are still extant. See *Collect. de Reb. Hib.* No. XIII. In the year 1252, O'Neil, an Irish chieftain, sent two hundred steeds with gold bitted bridles to O'Brien, another Irish chieftain. Vide *Ann. of Innisfallen.*

FIRE-ARMS

WERE unknown in Ireland till the reign of Henry VIII. " In the " year 1489, (says Harris) the first Musquets or Fire-Arms that " perhaps were ever seen in Ireland, were brought to Dublin from Ger- " many, and six of them, as a great rarity, were presented to Gerald, " earl of Kildare, then lord deputy, which he put into the hands of his " guards, as they stood centinels before his house in Thomas-court (*d*)." After this period, Fire-arms were no longer a rarity in this country: during the Elizabethan wars, they were liberally diffused through the kingdom. It was for the purpose of carrying on those wars with more terror to the natives, that pieces of ordnance were first introduced. At this time part of the Spanish Armada happening to be wrecked on the Irish coast, some of the Cannon were cast on shore. One of them is now preserved in the Armory of the Castle of Dublin, where it was deposited by colonel Vallancey, who had it brought up from Kinsale. In the same repository is preserved the cannon which killed saint Ruth; but being covered with ammunition carriages, I could not obtain a drawing of it. It is, I am told, a long six-pounder.

Thus, with a rapid hand, having completed my design, I shall dismiss this Memoir with a poetical adjunct. O'Hoefy, a modern Irish Bard, contrasting the ancient discipline of the Irish, with that of late days, exclaims with indignation.—

(*d*) *Hist. of Dub.* p 283.

Ní faicthear Gille angeall Treara.
Na trealamh laoich laimh re Cuilt;
Na colg ag deól deapnann laimhe.
Ní cheanglann reo fainne fuilt.

No more the foe now trembles at our name,
No more their captive numbers fwell our fame;
No martial earth is by the foldier preft,
The fword, the fole companion of his reft:
No warriors nightly canopy'd with air,
See the froft bind the ringlets of their hair;
Our weapons idly in our fcabbards ftand,
Nor grow, as erft, to ev'ry valiant hand.

POSTSCRIPT.

POSTSCRIPT.

THE greater part of this Memoir was worked off, when I was favoured by Mr. Grofe (the learned author of A Treatise on Ancient Armour and Weapons) with a drawing of a suit of Armour worn by an Irish earl in the reign of king John. This, I hope, will plead my pardon with Mr. Grofe for omitting to notice, in its proper place, his valuable communication.

While this sheet was in the prefs, William Mitchell, efq; (author of some curious pieces refpecting Irish antiquities, published anonymously at different times) informed me, that while a boy he happened to be prefent in the shop of one Moore, a silver-smith, near Skinner-row, Dublin, when a peafant offered for fale a golden helmet which he had found in the county of Tipperary. Caught with its glittering appearance, he was induced to examine it and to try it on his head. From the image of this helmet which remained impressed on his memory, he defcribed it as refembling in form a huntfman's cap, with the leaf in front divided equally and elevated. The fcull was encompaffed with a ribband of gold crimped.—Two bodies cafed in Armour were raifed in Dublin within Mr. Mitchel's recollection.

APPENDIX.

[No. I.]

AN

ACCOUNT

OF THE

CUSTOMS, MANNERS, AND DRESS

Of the Inhabitants of

THE ROSSES on the Coast of the County of DONEGAL,
IRELAND.

IN A LETTER TO THE AUTHOR.

APPENDIX.

AN ACCOUNT, &c.*

Dear Sir,

UNDERSTANDING that you would be glad of any authentic information respecting the native Irish; and, having been highly entertained with some curious anecdotes concerning the inhabitants of the islands called The Rosses, on the coast of Donegal; as a proof of my regard for you, I here present you with some particulars which I have collected, partly from the personal conversation, and partly from the literary correspondence of my worthy friend, Mr. N—— of the county of Donegal.

In the years 1753 and 1754 his brother, then an eminent attorney, prevailed on my friend to accompany a person employed to transact some law business at The Rosses; the people there being then deemed savage and unamenable

---

* As this letter contains a very curious account of the state of society in The Rosses, at the commencement of the present century, I was unwilling to do violence to the writer's narration, by suppressing such parts of it as do not immediately belong to my subject.

menable to law: and, accordingly, when they underſtood the purpoſe of the viſiſt, they aſſembled with determination to oppoſe its accompliſhment; and the expedition might have proved both fruitleſs and fatal, if Mr. N—— had not been maſter at once, both of their language and of his own temper; but by his prudence and good humour, he tempered their paſſion; while, by reaſoning with them in Iriſh, he convinced their underſtanding. From their ſubſequent demeanour it appeared, however, the fire which had heated their firſt indignation, had been kindled by generous principles, natural to the human heart: the love of liberty, averſion to change, and attachment to a former landlord.

During his reſidence among them, Mr. N—— had ample opportunities of obſervation, which he was prompted to attend to, no leſs by neceſſity, than by curioſity: on their firſt appearance, their Dreſs attracted his notice; the demands of nature forced him to obſerve their food, and his being accuſtomed to elegant accommodation at home, could not fail of exciting aſtoniſhment at their want of even decency in their manner of ſleeping.

Notwithſtanding their high latitude and bleak ſituation, none of them had more than two garments, and thoſe of flannel of their own manufacture; the men, a waiſtcoat and breeches, the women a gown and petticoat: but there was no linen in common uſe among them; neither did Mr. N—— ſee above three or four women, who wore ſhifts, ſhoes, or ſtockings; nor a ſingle man with any more than a waiſtcoat and breeches on him.

Notwithſtanding their ſeeming neglect of their perſons, thoſe iſlanders were not without a ſpice of vanity: for they had invented dye ſtuffs to diverſify the colours of their clothes; and their dying materials were (all of them) the produce of their own ſoil: the principal theſe three; a kind

of

APPENDIX.

of mud, called *Mire-black*, made a very deep and durable black; a kind of stuff called *Carker* scraped off the rocks, made a very fine red; and a kind of plant almost the same, and of the same effect as *Madder*. The men's clothes were of divers colours; but the women's dress was regularly uniform, black gowns with red petticoats: but there was a distinction observed in the head dress of the females. The maidens wore the front part of their hair neatly platted about the face; the rest hanging down long behind, in separate locks, platted with hair-lace, and adorned at the ends with worsted tassels of divers colours: but the matrons did not plat their hair, only tying it with a small string, below which they let it play loose upon their backs.

Their usual summer diet consisted of milk, curds, and butter, with most excellent fish of several kinds; in winter they lived on potatoes, fish, rabbits, and butter; and some of them, but very few, had a little bread, made of barley or oaten meal: but, though some used salt to save their provision of fish, they had none with their ordinary victuals; the want of which, with the scarcity of bread, at first made their food so uncomfortable to Mr. N—— that he rode several miles into the neighbouring country, and could hardly find a small supply for money. In one of the largest islands, called *Oiey*, they used to kill great numbers of Seals, the flesh of which they salted for winter; and were so fond of it, as to prefer it to any other kind of meat. When reconciled to Mr. N—— and pleased with his affability they became very friendly and kind; and there was every week a sheep bought for him, which cost but six or seven shillings, weighing from nine to eleven pounds the quarter, as good mutton as ever he ate; which, with rabbits, lobsters, crabs, scollops and oysters in abundance, made every meal a feast.

Their houses were but mere huts, consisting chiefly of one room, with the fire in the middle of it: but what surprized Mr. N—— most, was
their

their extraordinary mode of accommodation for the night's repose. All the family lay together in one bed; and, if any visitors came in the evening, they too slept with them; for they set no bounds to their hospitality. To provide lodging for the whole company, the youngest men were sent out for heath or bent-bushes; which they spread across the floor, to a length sufficient for the number present, and in breadth about six feet: over this litter, the mistress of the house laid part of a long plaid or blanket, on which the others, having stripped off their clothes, lay down as fast as they could; men and women together, all naked: then the mistress having drawn the rest of the blanket over them, lay down last herself, naked also. This they called a Thorough-bed, and Mr. N—— was perhaps the only person, who had ever before worn a shirt in it. Yet this hospitable people, so friendly and generous to those they knew, appeared at first to strangers to be wild and fierce; but, after a little acquaintance, proved gentle and humane, especially to those they were in awe of; for, in all their simplicity, there was a strong mixture of cunning.

They had very little industry among them; for, so well contented were they with the gifts of Providence, wherewith those islands are plentifully surrounded; they had no notion of any other necessaries of life, than what they already were used to; and had scarce a wish beyond the supply of the present moment: that being answered, their only care was to provide for their landlord; and to purchase spirits and tobacco, their only luxury, of which they were all, both men and women, excessively fond. In Summer therefore, the men gathered the wrack of Sea-weeds, and burned it to make kelp; of which, the landlord or his Agent got as much, as was rated equivalent to the rent; and, if any remained, it was bartered, for what they most wanted or most desired: the rest of the year the general and principal employment of the men was fishing, except what was necessary for their potatoes and clothing, or the repairs of their huts and boats.

Their

Their boats, called Curraghs, were oval baskets, covered with Seal-skins; and, in such weak and tottering vessels, they ventured so far out, as was necessary, to get fish enough for their families: but their shell-fish they got in the following manner; the men went to the rocks with a hook tied to the end of a strong rod; and with that they pulled from under the rocks, as many crabs and lobsters as they wanted; the lobsters commonly weighing from five to twelve pounds each: for scollops and oysters, when the tide was out, the young women waded into the sea where they knew the beds of such fish lay; some of them, naked; others having stripped off their petticoats, went in with their gowns tucked up about their waist; and, by armfulls, brought to shore, whatever number of scollops and oysters they thought requisite; the scollops weighing from two to four pounds each.

When the weather was favourable the women frequently assembled in some neighbouring field, convenient to their huts; where they amused themselves with knitting and singing in the Sun. The oldest, forming a circular group, sat working in the middle; round them, the rest in circles, according to their years; the younger surrounding those of greater age, and singing alternate, and sometimes in chorus, while the elder continued knitting. Their songs, called *Speic-Seoachs*, were recitals of exploits atchiev'd by the giants, and warriors, and hunters of old. (*) Here it obviously occurs as a matter of reasonable enquiry, what became

of

(*) This relation of my friend reminds me of the following passage in SHAKE-SPEAR's *Twelfth Night*,

——— The song we had last night———
Mark it Cesario, it is true and plain:
The spinsters and the knitters in the Sun,
And the free maids that weave their threads with bones,
Do use to chant it.

of all the stockings made by so many so often engaged in knitting, though none of them would (themselves) deign to wear any such thing: but, having no better authority to ground opinion upon, we may suppose, the females disposed of their handy-work, as the men did of their overplus of kelp, as necessity or gratification directed.

Their funeral processions were no less worthy of notice, than their other customs. Wrapped in a coarse woollen cloath, by them called *Ebed*, the corse was put into a Curragh, with the feet and legs hanging over the stern; and (with it) a man with a paddle, to conduct the whole train to the Isle of Aran, where their burial-ground was: this Curragh was followed by that, which carried the priest; next him went the relations of the deceased, in the order of their proximity in kindred; and then as many as had Curraghs; and of these, Mr. N—— saw sixty or eighty in a train.

When Mr. N—— returned to Dublin, it was necessary to bring some of the men with him from the Rosses; and he found it very difficult to get them dressed fit to appear in the Courts.—Yet these same Islanders so irreconcilable then to the modes of their civilized countrymen, in less than forty years became quite another kind of people, totally altered in their carriage and conduct, their habiliments and habitations, their occupations and manner of living; for, when Mr. N—— paid them a visit in 1787, he found them so much improved by their intercourse with others, that he scarce knew some of his old acquaintance; and was no less pleased than surprized at seeing spruce young lads fashionably dressed on Sundays, in sattin waistcoats and breeches, with white silk stockings, silver buckles, and ruffled shirts.

In

In converfation with an elderly gentleman, who had above forty years ago made the tour of North Britain, when I communicated what I had learned concerning The Roffes; he affured me, that my defcription of thefe Iflanders is an exact picture of what he had feen in the Scotch Highlands and the Orkney Iflands.

If what I have here fet down can be of any ufe to you, it is at your fervice, from

Your fincere friend and

Very humble fervant,

A———— B————,

DUBLIN,
April 10, 1788.

No. II.

[No. II.]

A

DESCRIPTIVE CATALOGUE

OF

IRISH IMPLEMENTS OF WAR, &c.

IN THE COLLECTION OF

RALPH OUSLEY, Esq. M. R. I. A.

IN A LETTER TO THE AUTHOR.

APPENDIX.

A DESCRIPTIVE CATALOGUE, &c.

Dear Sir,

IN your last favour you express a desire to know what kind and number of Irish warlike implements are in my collection. I now sit down, with much pleasure, to comply with your request; but must first observe, that having mislaid my catalogue, I fear I cannot be as satisfactory as either you or I could wish.—

A brass (or mixed metal) halbert, in good preservation, with three holes for rivets, and one brass rivet yet remaining. It is 8 inches long, and $2\frac{3}{4}$ broad; weighs $7\frac{1}{2}$ ozs. Found in Athlone in 1778.

An halbert (part of) $8\frac{1}{2}$ inches long, and 2 inches broad; weighs $7\frac{1}{4}$ ozs. Found near Dunmore, co. Galway, in 1781.

An halbert with a curve. It is $9\frac{1}{4}$ inches long, and $2\frac{1}{4}$ broad. Weighs 7 ozs. Found in Limerick, 1781.

APPENDIX.

An halbert with two rivets of brafs. It is 11 inches long, and 3½ broad. Weighs 11½ oz. Found near Athlone in 1782.

An halbert 10½ inches long, and 2¾ broad. Weighs 12 oz. Found near Limerick, in 1781.

Fourteen heads of Spears and Darts, from 2½ inches to 8½ inches long. And from 1½ to 7 oz. weight. Amongst these is a beautiful triangular Spear, with a screw, in fine prefervation, which was found near Ennis in the county of Clare in 1786. It is 7 inches long, and weighs 6¼ oz.

A fword (the hilt broken) found in the co. of Clare, near Limerick, in 1782. It is 15½ inches long, and weighs 14 ozs.

A beautiful fword found at Raigh, near Dunmore, co. Galway, in 1774. It is 23¼ inches long, and weighs 1lb. 6 oz.

Thirteen Celts, from 2 to 12½ oz.

Eleven fpurs from 1 to 4 oz. Some of the rowels more than 2½ inches, diameter.

Eleven Tuagh-Suaighte, or Chipping-axes, from 6 oz. to 1lb. and upwards; and different from any exhibited or mentioned in No. XIII. of COLLECT. DE REB. HIB.—Five of thefe Axes weigh from 6 oz. to 2lb. 2 ozs.

Several Broches of brafs, filver, and gold; and gold and filver mixed.

I have

I have also chain rings, bodkins, Druidical scythes, images, gouges, trumpets, and many other brass antiquities, but rather foreign to your present enquiry.

    I am,

      Dear Sir,

        With great truth,

          Your faithful and obedient servant,

              RALPH OUSLEY.

WILLSBOROUGH,
CASTLEREA,
April 4, 1788.

[No. III.]

AN ACCOUNT OF THREE RELICKS OF ANTIQUITY FOUND IN IRELAND.

APPENDIX.

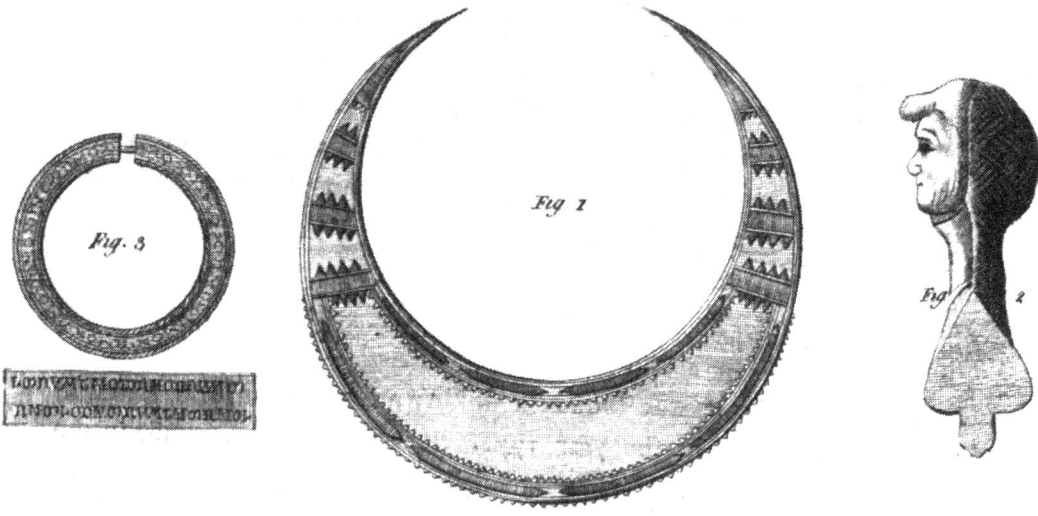

An Account of three RELICKS of ANTIQUITY found in IRELAND.

FIG. I.

THIS curious relick was lately found on the lands of Kilwarlin, in the county of Down, and is now in the poffeffion of the right honourable the earl of Hillfborough, who politely communicated the drawing. It is made of a thin plate of gold. In form, it is nearly circular, (as reprefented above), the diameter about 8 inches; and the rim, in the broadeft part, 2¼ inches.

Concerning

Concerning the use of this implement, I shall not venture to offer a decided opinion. By some it is supposed to have been worn as a collar or gorget; by others, it is considered as an ornament for the head. (See above, page 9.) It is certainly of too small a compass to encircle the neck; but might be worn on the head or breast. Ignorant of the real use of this implement, conjecture might betray me into inconsistency; I shall therefore commit it to the antiquary to dispose of as he may think fit.

Fig. II.

Is made of brass; It was found in sinking a foundation for a house in Church-street, Dublin, in the year 1772. It remained for a while in the collection of the reverend Mervyn Archdall, whence it passed into that of the right honourable W. Conynghame. The singularity of the head-dress obtained for it a place here.

Fig. III.

A golden ring or Amulet, found in the ruins of a castle in the county of Wicklow. It is now in the possession of Arthur Wolfe, esquire. Having consulted a learned friend, concerning the probable use of this ring, and the legend with which it is inscribed, he favoured me with the following attempt.

" I here send an attempt to explain the Amulet, but am not very certain that I have found the true reading. It is inscribed with Gothic letters of the 14th and 15th centuries, which letters were derived from the Runic of the 11th century, several of which are contained in this Inscription. It appears to have been a pardon, or absolution-seal belonging to a priest or confessor of the Cavanagh family.

APPENDIX. 161

On one fide is,

Iomachaith matmhiachaithiac machaith a mhac o mhac chaithmhanachaith.

For,

Iomhadhaogh maithmheachaithiac machuibh a mhac o mac chaomhanachaibh.

That is,

Multitudes of pardons to the fons of the fon of Mc. Cavanaghs.

On the reverfe,

Mac o mac o mac mac o mac o mac o mac o mac o m.

The fon from the fon from the fon's fon from the fon from the fon from the fon from the fons, &c. that is, from one generation to another, for ever."

" Thefe kind of indulgences, were common during the dark periods of the latter ages; they were given by the popes and legates to abbots, priors, and confeffors, for the ufe of their patrons and great families, who, no doubt, paid well for them. They were either given in metal, to be worn pendent on their bofoms; or by impreffions on wax, to be worn in a cafe: feveral have been found in England, in the Runic, Gothic, and Latin characters, and in the Latin and Saxon languages. This under confideration, does not appear older than the 15th century."

" This infcription perhaps was intended to have been read alfo backwards, as moft of the Runic legends or amulets found in England are;

X indeed

indeed, almoſt all Runic inſcriptions of ſhort ſentences are generally read backwards as well as forwards, and were conſidered amongſt the unenlightened, as charms."

I ſhall here take occaſion to obſerve, that in no nation were charms more prevalent than in Ireland. In the dark ages they were worn on every occaſion. In the time of Camden, the Kern never went to the field of battle without his Amulet. Even at this day, the Iriſh peaſantry conſider the little Arrow-heads of ſtone, which are found in ſuch abundance in this kingdom, as being endued with a ſecret charm, and accordingly wear them about their neck as an Amulet, frequently ſetting them in ſilver. Shakeſpear alludes to the popular belief of the power of magic in Ireland, in As you like it. Act 3, Scene 6. It is alſo hinted at by Randolph, another early Engliſh poet.

[No. IV.]

[No. IV.]

AN

ACT,

THAT THE

SUBJECTS OF THIS REALME

SHALL HAVE

BOWES AND OTHER ARMOUR.

(10 HEN. VII.)

An Act that the Subjects of this Realme shall have Bowes and other Armour.

(10 *Hen.* VII.)

ITEM, prayen the commons, that in consideration that the subjects of Ireland have none English bowes and arrowes for the resistence of malice of their enemies and rebels, like as they have had in times passed; by reason whereof they be not so able to defend them from destruction, as they were at other seasons heretofore: therefore it be ordeyned, enacted, and established by authority of this present Parliament, That every subject having goods and cattels to the value of X. li. have an English bow and a sheaf of arrowes according; every subject having goods to the value of XX. li. have a jack salett, an English bow a sheafe of arrowes; every freeholder, having land to the value yearely of foure pounds, have his horse, jack salett, bow and sheaf of arrowes; every lord, knight, and esquire, within the said land have for every yeoman daily in their houshold, Jack Salett, Bow, and Arrowes, to the intent that all the commons of the said land may be able to doe the King or his Lieutenant service for their own defence and surety.

II. And by the same authority it be ordeyned, That if the foresaid persons, or any of them, doe not observe and perform the premisses as it is before

fore specified, that then they and every of them doe forfeit to the King, Vi s. Viii d. as oftentimes as they and every of them shall offend the foresaid ordinance.

III. And by the same authority it be ordeyned, That there be henceforward in every barony within every shire of the said land two wardens of peace, having authority as it hath bin used of old time, and in every parish constables of able persons inhabitants within the said parishes, and a payre of Butts to be had within every of the foresaid parishes, at the cost of the said parishioners, that the commons of the said land may the sooner attain the practise and experience of Archers; and that the foresaid constables in every parish upon pain of forfeiture of xiid. at every default, doe call before them or one of them every haly day all and every of the foresaid persons, having Bowes and Arrowes, as afore is rehearsed, to shoot, and cause them to shoot, at the least, two or three games at the said Butts.

IV. And by the same authority it be ordeyned, That if any of the said persons make default at any haly day, without a reasonable cause shewed, that then the said constables have full power and authority to record their defaults, and amerce them and every of them at every such default in iiiid. and the saide constables to present the said amerciaments in writing to the barons of the King's exchequer in the said land, to be levied and perceived in like maner and forme as the King's revenues been levied there.

[No. V.]

[No. V.]

LIST

OF THE

PLATES

WHICH ILLUSTRATE THIS WORK;

WITH

OBSERVATIONS.

APPENDIX.

LIST of the PLATES which illuftrate this Work, with OBSERVATIONS.

FRONTISPIECE.

I Cannot better explain this elegant little defign than in the words of him whofe fancy conceived it. " It reprefents two Irifh warriors on the con-
" fines of a wood. The figure on the left is armed with the fourteen-feet
" Pike and the Battle-axe, and cloathed in the thrum Jacket and clofe
" Truife: on his head is the Monteraro cap, worn by the Irifh infantry in
" the 15th and 16th centuries, as appears from a drawing in the College, re-
" prefenting the taking of the earl of Defmond by O'Conor. The head of
" this figure is after an head of an Irifh foldier given in the original Latin
" edition of Ware. Behind the figure hangs his wicker Shield and Skein.
" The figure on the right is cloathed in the Dhilimor, without Truife or
" Slieves, with the cloak as defcribed by Froiffart. On his head is the coni-
" cal cap, taken from a figure in the Black-abbey, Kilkenny. In his left
" hand he holds his Staff, and in his right the fhort fcuit or Dart; behind
" him, on the rock, lies his wicker Shield and heavy Sword. The Shields
" are taken from Cordiner, and the Sword from the Crofs of St. Boyne.
" In the middle, at a diftance, rides a chief throwing his Lance, clad in the
" Dhilimor and Canabhas, covering his head and all the body. This figure
" is taken from that of M'Murrough meeting the earl of Gloucefter, in the
" Harleian MSS. In the back ground are mountains and a round tower."

Plate I. (p. 4.)

Fig. 1. was sketched by Mr. Beauford of Athy, from a Stone-cross at Clonemacnoise. Fig. 2, 3. were taken by the same gentleman from the shaft of a Cross digged up in the church-yard of Old Kilcullen, in the county of Kildare. Fig. 4. drawn by Mr. Beauford also. Fig. 5. copied from an engraving in the 7th vol. of the ARCHÆOLOGIA. Fig. 6. sketched by the rev. D. A. Beauford, from a monument at Strade in the county of Mayo.

Plate II. (p. 15.)

Fig. 1, 2. Fibulæ, taken by col. Vallancey from the originals still extant. (See p. 5. Fig. 3. a Fibula in the collection of R. Ousley, esq; drawn by W. Ousley, esq. Fig. 4, 5. Bodkins, from drawings taken by col. Vallancey from the originals.

Plate III. (p. 22.)

Fig. 1, 2, 3. regal figures from fresco-paintings at Knockmoy, county of Galway. The drawing from whence these figures were copied, was executed by Mr. Wm. Leeson, in the year 1784. Fig 4. a Druid's crown as given in pag. 70. of COLLECT. DE REB. HIB. Fig. 5. a golden crown supposed to be still extant in France.

Plate IV. (p. 29.)

This drawing was made at my request in the year 1787, by Wm. Ousley esq; who had the scattered fragments of the monument collected for the purpose. This monument (which exhibits both the religious and military habits

APPENDIX.

habits of the times) was erected to the memory of Felim O'Conor, King of Munster, and nephew of the unfortunate Roderic, in the year 1265. He is reprefented in a monaftic habit, with an otter at his feet. This monument was much damaged by a party of Cromwell's foldiers. A few years fince, the figures of the Galloglaffes were pulled down in a drunken frolic.

Plate V. (p. 34.)

Fig. 1, 2. Irifh kings in their robes. Fig. 1. was fketched from a Crofs at Monafter-boice, by Mr. W. Beauford. Fig. 2. taken from a monument at Strade, in the county of Mayo, in the year 1787, by the rev. D. A. Beaufort. This figure, and fig. 6. in Plate I. were prepared for the engraver by Mr. J. Maginnis. Fig. 3, 4. Bodkins, fee p. 15. Fig. 5, a Bodkin in the poffeffion of the countefs of Granard.

Plate VI. (p. 39.)

A female figure on a monument in the abbey of Athaffel, in the county of Limerick. Drawn on the fpot by Mr. A. Cooper, in the year 1781.

Plate VII. (p. 43.)

A female figure in St. Mary's church at Howth. Drawn on the fpot by my Brother, in the year 1787.

Plate VIII. (p. 46.)

Fig. 1, 2. Female figures on a monument at Old Kilcullen, in the county of Kildare. Drawn by Mr. W. Beauford.

APPENDIX.

Plate IX. (p. 48.)

Female figure on a monument at Fertagh, in the co. of Kilkenny. Drawn by Mr. A. Cooper, in 1781.

Plate X. (p. 58.)

Fig. 1, 2. Copied on a large scale, by my Brother, from A MAP OF THE TAKING OF THE EARL OF ORMOND, amongst the M. S. S. of Trinity College, Dublin. Permission to have this map copied was politely granted me by the board of Fellows. A copy is now in my possession, from one made by col. Vallancey.

Plate XI. (p. 68.)

The figures in this plate were taken by Mr. Gore Ousley, (now of Calcutta) from a sketch of the tomb by an accomplished young lady of the family of Aylmer.

Tail-piece, (p. 94.)

This drawing was made from the windows of the upper Treasury, by Mr. A. Cooper, in the year 1782.—The range of little buildings that appear to cover the base of the tower have been lately removed.

Plate XII. (p. 110.)

Fig. 1. a knight templar taken by my Brother from a tomb at Lusk, county of Dublin. Fig. 2. a knight in chain-mail, taken by Mr. A. Cooper, from a monument at old Kilcullen, county Kildare, supposed to be one of the family of the Eustaces. I was sorry, not long since, to see the stone on which

this

APPENDIX.

this figure is sculptured, removed from its place, and resting against the walls of the church. Fig. 3, 4, 5. little figures taken from the MAP OF THE TAKING OF THE EARL OF ORMOND, and given for the purpose of shewing the Glib, Pike, and manner of caparisoning an horse at that period, (1601.) Fig. 6. an Archer, from the fresco-paintings at Knockmoy.

Plate XIII. (p. 127.)

Fig. 1. A two-handed sword in the castle of Howth, 5 feet 7¼ inches long. Fig. 2. a beautiful spear-head of brass, 2½ inches long. Fig. 3. an iron sword found at Kilmainham, and conjectured to have belonged to a knight templar. Its length 3 feet and one inch. Fig. 4. a small battle-axe of iron, in the collection of the countess of Moira, the spear part broken off. It is 4 inches long. Fig. 5. a sword found in the bog of Cullen, county of Tipperary. Fig. 6. a skein. Fig. 7. a battle-axe, from a sketch of some rude pieces of sculpture on the bridge of Athlone. Fig. 8. a spear-head of stone. In the SAGGI DI DISS. ACCAD. DELLA ACCAD. ETRUSCA DI CORTONA, is given an engraving of the head of a weapon, there called a lance, closely resembling this figure. Diss. v. tav. 2. Fig. 9. a small iron battle-axe found with fragments of other iron weapons, and some human bones, on the lands of Barnhall, county Kildare. It is 7 inches long, and 5¼ inches broad. Fig. 10. the battle-axe, carried at this day by the battle-axe guard of the castle of Dublin.

FINIS.

ADDENDA ET CORRIGENDA.

AS the author never means to refume the fubjects treated of in this little Work, he here fubjoins a few notices fuggefted by his memory and his friends, fince the laft fheets were ejected by the prefs. He alfo avails himfelf of this opportunity of correcting a few errors, which had efcaped his obfervation when he firft read the work with a view to *errata*. Yet the eye of Criticifm, no doubt, will difcover many deficiencies ftill unfupplied, and many errors ftill uncorrected. But perfection, unattainable by the ableft literary veteran, muft be very far removed from the reach of a young author, of flender abilities and various avocations.

Page 10. Line 6. We may therefore venture to give the Brog or Brogue to the early Irifh.

GUILLIM informs us, that the ancient family of Arthur of Ireland, beareth Gules, a chevron between three *Irifh Brogues or*.—Vide *Difp. of Herald.* p. 301.

Page 27. Line 6. It fhould feem that the Irifh, as it were in a fit of defpair, put off all their finery on the approach of the Englifh, &c.

It may be inferred from a paffage in *The Annals of Innisfallen* (MS.) that the Queens of the Irifh reguli, in the reign of Hen. II. adorned their perfons with glittering and coftly ornaments; for we are told by our Annalift, that when Dearbhghuall, the wife of O'Ruairc, King of Conmhaine, was taken prifoner in the year 1152, her *trinkets and jewels* became the prey of the enemy.

P. 39.

ADDENDA ET CORRIGENDA.

P. 39. Line 7.

Reticulated, *potius* braided.

P. 45. Note *(x)*. The Veil was in general use amongst the early Irish.

The Veil is mentioned in some ancient Brehon Laws under the name of *Fele* or *Fiadhail*.

P. 47. Note *(f)*.

For Holinghed *r.* Holinshed.

P. 55. Line 12. Nor is he a greater friend to the Glibbs.

A writer of the reign of Elizabeth, thus mentions the Glibb, in speaking of the wild Irish.—" Proud they are of long crisped bushes of heare which they terme Glibbs, and the same they nourish with all their cunning, to crop the front thereof they take it for a notable piece of villanie." HOLINSHED's *Chron of Irel.*

P. 74. Line 14.

For county *r.* country.

Ibid. Note *(u)*. Love and a Bottle.

I should, perhaps, have observed, that the passages in this comedy which I have cited, fall from a young Irishman.

P. 106.

ADDENDA ET CORRIGENDA.

P. 106. Line 19. Their inflexible attachment to their civil Dress,
&c.

Mr. O'Conor informs me, he has seen several Irish poems which were evidently written with a view of dissuading the Irish from adopting the Armour as well as the civil Dress of the English. And in our Annals we often find the Irish marching to the field of battle in their Mantles, long after the English invasion.

P. 113. Line 12. It is however a well attested fact, that a golden Shield, or rather a Shield adorned with gold, was found not many years since near Lismore, &c.

Although the principal fact of this curious discovery was strongly impressed on my informant's memory, there remained but imperfect traces of the attending circumstances; he therefore recommended it to me to apply for the several particulars to Richard Gumbleton, esq; of Lismore, the source whence his knowledge was drawn. An hasty and an unexpected call to the Continent preventing Mr. Gumbleton from resolving my enquiry, his brother (W. C. Gumbleton, esq;) kindly and politely undertook to obtain for, and furnish me with the information I requested. "As to the fact (says he, in a letter which I re-
" ceived while this sheet was in the press) it is certain a gold Shield (or rather a Corselet)
" was found in a small coppice near my brother's house about seventy years since, and
" sold for 600l. to a gold-smith at Cork, whose name cannot at present be learned. The
" Shield or Corselet answers the description of an entire covering for the body, beginning
" at the neck, terminating at the hips and closing behind with three clasps; but
" whether it was plain gold, done in relief, or merely engraved, I cannot satisfy
" myself."

P. 117.

P. 117. Line 21. I cannot find that the Irish warriors, like the heroes of the Round-Table, distinguished their swords by proper names.

Although such a custom eluded my research, it is not improbable that it prevailed amongst the early Irish; for the Celtic poets, who are generally faithful to the manners of the times, distinguish the Swords of their heroes by certain names or epithets. See p. 58, 210. of *Scan Dana le Oiffan, Orran, Ullan*, by the ingenious Dr. SMITH, a gentleman to whom Celtic literature has many obligations.

P. 119. Line 3. As well in Ireland as in England, and on the Continent, the Dagger, &c.

Dr. Smith in his *Nat. and Civ. Hist. of Cork*, gives the figure of an ancient Irish weapon of the Dagger-kind, called Dadagh, which he tells us is in the possession of O'Donovan of Banlaghan, and reserved as an heir-loom in the family. It was taken by an ancestor of O'Donovan, from one of the Clancarty family in a bloody contest, near the castle of Blarney The doctor describes it as resembling an Highland Dirk and Spanish Miquelet. Vol. II. p. 414.

P. 120. Line 18. A brass Spear-head of an elegant form, &c.

This is the only Spear-head with eyes found in Ireland, that has fallen under my observation. Yet Spear-heads so formed were not uncommon amongst the ancient Irish. In the old romances the usual epithet for the Spear is, *Slidh cheann-ramhar chro-fhairsing catha*; that is, *the heavy-headed, broad-eyed Spear of battle.*

P. 125.

ADDENDA ET CORRIGENDA.

P. 125.

For ufed this *r.* ufed the.

P. 132. Line 10. The laft member of this Club (the Archers') &c.

Several copies of this work had paffed into the world before I was made acquainted with the prefent exiftence of a member of The Archers' Club. The perfon to whom I allude is Mr. Richard Cave, of Paradife-row, Dublin, an amiable old man, with whom I have fince converfed, with much pleafure, on the practice of Archery in his time. The total diffolution of the Club, he informs me, did not happen till the year 1745, when the members joining the Militia then raifed, were eftranged from the practice of Archery by the new exercife impofed on them. Two of the Bows, feveral of the Arrows, and one of the Quivers which belonged to this Club, are in the poffeffion of Mr. Cave. One of the Bows was imported from the Weft Indies; the other (which is made of yew) from a town in the neighbourhood of Warrington, (England,) whence the Club were ufually fupplied: they are both about fix feet long. Mr. Cave has no doubt of his being the laft living member of the Club.

P. 135. Line 2.

For Henry VIII. *r.* Henry VII.

P. 144. Line 2.

For vifift. *r.* vifit.

P. 162.

ADDENDA ET CORRIGENDA.

P. 162. Line 7. Even at this day, the Irish peasantry consider the little Arrow-heads of stone, which are found in such abundance in this kingdom, as being endued with a secret charm.

When a beast happens to pine or nauseate its food, the vulgar Irish conclude, that the animal has been smote by the hand of a fairy, with one of these darts; whence they are commonly called Elf-darts: This superstition, which also prevails in Scotland, is happily alluded to by COLLINS, in a fine Ode lately rescued from oblivion.

"There every herd, by sad experience knows
 How, wing'd with fate, their *Elf-shot Arrows* fly;
When the sick ewe her summer food foregoes,
Or, stretch'd on earth, the heart-smit heifers lie."

Transf. of the Roy. Soc. of Edinb. Part. 2. p. 68.

P. 169. Line 13, 20.

For Dhilimor *r.* Foilmean, (a folded garment.)

P. 171. Line 2.

For Munster, *r.* Connaught.

Ibid. Line 3. An otter at his feet.

I am informed that there are several monumental figures in different parts of this kingdom with an Otter at the feet.

P. 171. Line 5.

For was *r.* were.

Ibid. Line 11.

For Maginnis *r.* Maguire,

www.ingramcontent.com/pod-product-compliance
Lightning Source LLC
Chambersburg PA
CBHW081352160426
43192CB00013B/2389